Living with uncertainty

The School Mathematics Project

CAMBRIDGE
UNIVERSITY PRESS

Main authors	Chris Belsom	With contributions from
	Stan Dolan	Robert Black
	Chris Little	David Cundy
	Mary Rouncefield	Jackie Gallard
		Howard Gilbert
		Sarah Lightfoot
		Fiona McGill
		Paul Roder

Team Leader   Chris Belsom

Project Director   Stan Dolan

Statistics program   Margaret and Peter Hayball

The authors would like to give their thanks to Ann White for her help in producing the trial edition and in preparing this book for publication.

The publishers would like to thank the following for permission to use copyright material:

text on pages 4 and 36 – from *Revised English Bible*, Oxford University Press and Cambridge University Press, 1989;

photographs on page 6   – AIP Meggers Gallery of Nobel Laureates;
                          Ann Ronan Picture Library;
photograph on page 7   – Dr Seth Shostak/Science Photo Library;
photograph on page 25 – Simon Fraser/Coronary Care Unit, Freeman Hospital, Newcastle/Science Photo Library;
photograph on page 73 – Stephen Dalton/NHPA.

Published by the Press Syndicate of the University of Cambridge
The Pitt Building, Trumpington Street, Cambridge CB2 1RP
40 West 20th Street, New York, NY 10011–4211, USA
10 Stamford Road, Oakleigh, Melbourne 3166, Australia

First published 1991
Third printing 1994

Printed in Great Britain at the University Press, Cambridge

Produced by Gecko Limited, Bicester, Oxon

Cover design by Iguana Creative Design

British Library cataloguing in publication data
16–19 mathematics.
Living with uncertainty
1. Statistical mathematics
I. School Mathematics Project
519.5

ISBN 0 521 38846 5 Paperback

Contents

Statistics and probability

1.1 Introduction

If the study of statistics is no more than the collection of data, then it can be considered to have had a long history. The *Domesday-book* of William the Conqueror is an early example of a good attempt to collect information about a population. *The Bible* provides evidence of even earlier examples, like the following from the *New Testament*

> In those days a decree was issued by the emperor Augustus for a census to be taken throughout the Roman world.
>
> Luke 2:1

Such enumerations are still practised today and a national census of the population is conducted in the United Kingdom every ten years. The ready availability of statistics of this kind helps to keep us informed of trends and changes in society which might influence our thinking and behaviour. It is important to be able to 'read' statistical information, for example about the dangers of smoking or about the association of heart disease with certain life styles, and to make informed judgements upon it. Your study of statistics should help you to do this.

> How could a headteacher find out how many pupils in her school smoked regularly? What difficulties might be encountered in collecting the data?

One of the early statisticians, better known for her other activities and achievements, was Florence Nightingale (1820–1910). As part of her efforts to improve the conditions for patients, she collected data in various hospitals on the causes of death and illness. She realised that it was always necessary to **use** and **interpret** information after it had been collected.

> The War Office has some of the finest statistics in the world. What comes of them? Little or nothing. Why? Because the Heads do not know how to make anything of them . . . What we want is not so much an accumulation of facts, as to teach the men who are to govern the country the use of statistical facts.
>
> Florence Nightingale

It is, of course, the **interpretation** of statistics that is at the heart of much controversy. Everyone knows the harsh reference to statistics made by Disraeli:

There are lies, damned lies and statistics.

Daily newspapers are a regular source of statistical information. Data is collected, published and commented upon in connection with just about everything imaginable. People's eating habits, road accidents, crime and cricket all come in for statistical analysis by the press.

TASKSHEET 1 — Regional trends (page 10)

Statistics is not the aimless collection of data for its own sake, or simply for general interest. The collection of data is normally made in response to a problem that needs to be investigated or to a hypothesis that is to be tested. It is the **collection** and **analysis** of data, followed by the making of **judgements, decisions** or **inferences**, which form the subject-matter of statistics. This can be summarised in the following way:

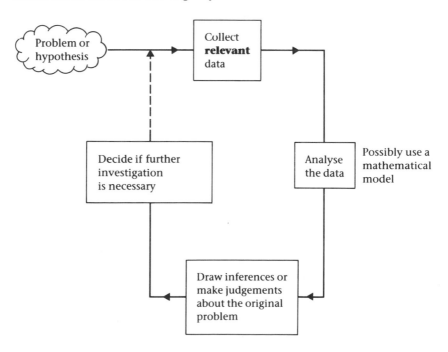

The study of statistics will involve you in a consideration of each of the areas mentioned in the chart. Projects and your own statistical investigations will give you the opportunity to engage in the full cycle of a statistical enquiry.

1.2 Order from chaos

Statistics and probability might appear to have applications only in the social sciences and not in the natural, physical world. The quotations below give an indication that probability is also profoundly important in the physical and biological sciences.

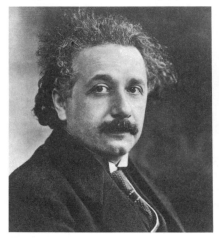

Gott würfelt nicht.
(God does not play dice.)
Albert Einstein

Whence comes all that order and beauty we see in the world?
Isaac Newton

In current theories about the behaviour of small particles, of the origin of the universe and of life on our planet (and elsewhere!) the idea of chance looms large. Richard Feynman, one of the greatest theoretical physicists of this century, wrote:

> . . . what we are proposing is that there is probability all the way back: that in the fundamental laws of physics there are odds.
>
> *The Character of Physical Law*, Richard Feynman, MIT Press, 1977

The emergence of ideas of chance into basic physical laws started with the kinetic theory of gases in the nineteenth century and continued in this century with the development of quantum mechanics.

> In general, quantum mechanics does not predict a single definite result for an observation. Instead, it predicts a number of different possible outcomes and tells us how likely each of these is.
>
> *A Brief History of Time*, Stephen Hawking, Bantam Press, 1988

Chance also plays a large part in biology.

> The Essence of life is statistical improbability on a colossal scale.
>
> *The Blind Watchmaker*, Richard Dawkins, Longman, 1986

Ideas of probability are fundamental to our understanding of the nature of life, of evolution and of the creation and behaviour of matter.

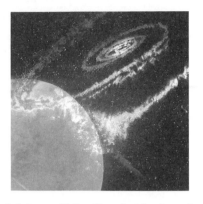

In the nineteenth century James Clerk Maxwell (in Cambridge) and Ludwig Boltzmann (in Austria) first introduced the ideas of randomness and chance events into the laws of physics with the kinetic theory of gases. They pictured a gas as a vast collection of individual molecules, rushing around chaotically in different directions and at different speeds, colliding with each other and with the walls of the container.

A simple experiment on gases which involves basic ideas of probability is to take a jar containing two gases which are distinguishable (for example by colour). The gases are initially separated by a barrier.

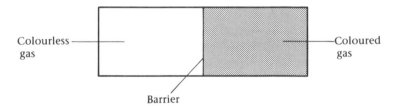

The barrier is removed and the gases mix freely. There will soon be molecules of each gas in each half of the jar. To understand why this happens consider a simplified situation in which there are only four molecules.

Each molecule moves around the jar in a random fashion; sometimes it will be in the left half of the jar and sometimes in the right. The possible distributions are shown in this table.

Number of molecules on the left	Number of molecules on right
4	0
3	1
2	2
1	3
0	4

To assess the probabilities of the five possible distributions it is helpful to 'label' the molecules. There is only one distribution with all molecules on the left:

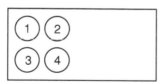

> You are not interested in the exact position of a molecule, only in whether it is in the left or the right side.

whereas there are four cases of a 3:1 split:

> Illustrate the four cases.

and six cases of a 2:2 split:

> With four molecules, how many different cases are there altogether?

The probability that there are equal numbers on both sides of the box is $\frac{6}{16}$ and this is the most likely state for the system.

Though the 2:2 split is the most likely, you will see that each of the others is possible. In a real experiment with a very large number of molecules, although all conceivable states are possible, you can show by a similar argument that each side is likely to contain roughly equal numbers of each type of molecule.

Despite the continuous motion of each molecule, the overall state remains roughly constant. The system is said to be in dynamic equilibrium.

The ideas of probability and statistics are now firmly embedded in all kinds of scientific study. In turn, some of the greatest scientists, by applying these ideas, have furthered our understanding of probability and statistics.

A reading list is provided in the unit guide and it is hoped that you will read at least parts of some of the books over the course of your studies. Additional reading will enrich your understanding of probability and statistics and enlarge upon the ideas introduced in the earlier discussion, helping to give you some insight into the range of applications of the subject.

 TASKSHEET 2 — Press release (page 12)

After working through this chapter you should:

1 be conscious of the wide-ranging importance of probability in the natural world;

2 be aware of the importance of statistical information, its impact and influence on the planning and organisation of our lives and the insights it gives into the way we live;

3 appreciate that statistics involves the four stages of:

> collecting relevant data,
> analysing the data,
> making inferences,
> deciding if a further investigation is necessary.

Regional trends

The following diagrams were reproduced in a national newspaper from the government publication *Regional Trends* (1988).

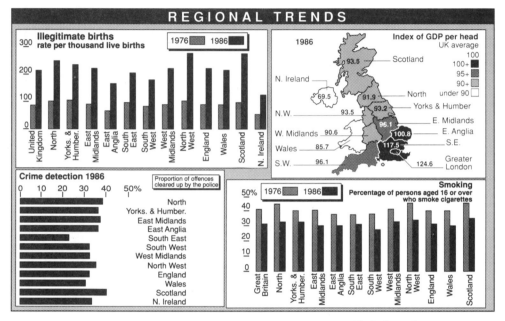

The Independent: 9 June 1988

Study the diagrams and then answer the questions based on this material.

1   In 1976, approximately what percentage of all births in the United Kingdom were described (in the diagram) as illegitimate?

What is the corresponding figure for 1986?

In 1986, which part of the UK registered the greatest and which the least percentage of illegitimate births?

2   The average gross domestic product (GDP) for the UK is fixed at 100. Figures for the regions are given in relation to this figure.

(a) What is the average GDP for those living in:

(i) Greater London;

(ii) Northern Ireland.

(b) Comment on any regional differences in GDP.

3 In 1986 the South East had the worst 'clearance' rate for criminal offences.

(a) What percentage of crimes was cleared up by the police in:

(i) the South East;

(ii) Scotland;

(iii) the North?

(b) Does the table give you any information about the numbers of crimes committed in these regions?

(c) How do you think data on:

(i) the clear up rate;

(ii) the number of crimes could be collected?

Do you see any problems?

4 The Government decides to launch a new anti-smoking campaign.

(a) Is there any evidence in the table for directing the advertising to particular regions?

(b) What other information on smoking habits might be useful in advising the Government on how to conduct its campaign?

Press release

You are commissioned to write a short article (of about 200 to 400 words) based on recently published data concerning illegitimate births in the United Kingdom. Some of the data are reproduced below. Study the data carefully and write the article. It should include comments on:

(a) the trend through this century to the present time (you might note and comment on the two peaks in 1918 and 1940–50);

(b) any regional differences;

(c) how the 'mother's age' has been changing over the more recent past.

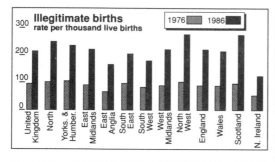

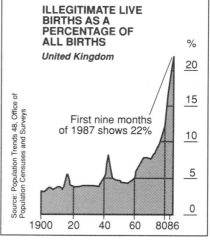

Illegitimate births by age of mother, England and Wales

Mother's age	1974 (%)	1986 (%)	% change 1974–1986
Under 16	1,553 (2.8%)	1,362 (1%)	−1.8%
16-19	19,308 (35.2%)	38,251 (27.1%)	−8.1%
20-24	17,568 (32%)	54,079 (38.3%)	+6.3%
25-29	9,950 (18.1%)	27,712 (19.6%)	+1.5%
All ages	54,891	141,345	+38.8%

The Independent: 9 & 13 June 1988

2 Exploratory data analysis

2.1 Introduction

Many statistical studies are prompted by debatable issues. Is there a connection between lung cancer and smoking? Are men worse drivers than women? Does lead in petrol affect the mental development of children?

In order to answer questions of this kind you need to collect data, analyse it and then draw conclusions.

Read the two articles below, both of which are about the 'Neighbourhood Watch' scheme of crime prevention.

NEIGHBOURHOOD WATCH

Local crime can be reduced.

Already around 20,000 Neighbourhood Watch Schemes have been established throughout Britain, helping to cut crime by up to 40% in their areas.

·That helps everyone – and people helping each other to cut crime is what Neighbourhood or Home Watch Schemes are all about. Everybody keeps an eye out for anything suspicious in the neighbourhood. And they are better informed about what to do if they see anything suspicious.

There's no great mystery about why the scheme has been successful.

'Crime watch' scheme flops

by Brian Deer
Social Affairs
Correspondent

NEIGHBOURHOOD watch, centrepiece of the government's crime-prevention strategy, is a failure, according to research commissioned by the Home Office and backed by Scotland Yard. Such schemes, which involve more than 4m people, have no effect on crime levels and possibly make them worse.

The findings are the result of a two-year investigation of neighbourhood watch carried out for the government at the Institute of Criminology in Cambridge. They include:

● Crime levels went up in the watch areas studied, while crime fell slightly in monitored areas that had no scheme. Both measurements are of crimes committed, not just those reported to police, and were collected by detailed questioning.

● Co-operation between police and public, measured by reported crime figures and by information telephoned to stations, showed no improvement in the watch areas. There was no rise in notification of suspicious persons.

The Sunday Times © Times Newspapers Ltd

Both of the above, contradictory, articles claim statistical backing! A study of statistics should help you to achieve a better and more critical understanding of the many statistical arguments which you will see and hear being used in debate.

How might you decide if a Neighbourhood Watch Scheme in your area was successful? What data would you collect?

The two-year investigation at the Institute of Criminology and many other experiments and surveys produce large amounts of data. The UK census conducted every ten years also yields a wealth of data of interest to economists, social scientists and geographers. Such information will eventually be used to make decisions which affect people's lives – for example how many hospital beds to provide for a city, whether there is a need for new road systems, etc.

During the course of your work in statistics you will conduct various experiments and surveys and analyse the results. As part of your work in other subjects you may collect data of your own, either as experimental results in physics, chemistry, biology or psychology, or survey work in geography or sociology; or you may analyse results collected by other people and published as official statistics. Data you collect yourself are known as **primary data**, whereas data collected by other people are called **secondary data.**

In most cases it is useful to have methods available for exploring the data and looking for possible patterns and trends before any detailed statistical analysis begins. Pictorial representations of data are often used to convey important features of the information rapidly.

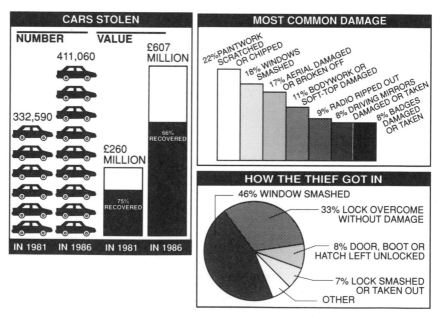

Car Security, *Which?*: March 1988

In recent years, new techniques known as Exploratory Data Analysis (EDA) have been developed. These make it possible to organise sets of data rapidly so that patterns can be spotted easily. The techniques of EDA are covered in this chapter, prior to the more detailed methods of statistical analysis of chapter 3.

2.2 Stem and leaf display

The White family are trying to decide where to spend their July holidays. Ann White argues for Torquay, whereas John favours going to Bournemouth. They decide to go to the resort with the better temperature record.

Much data on the weather are available in newspapers.

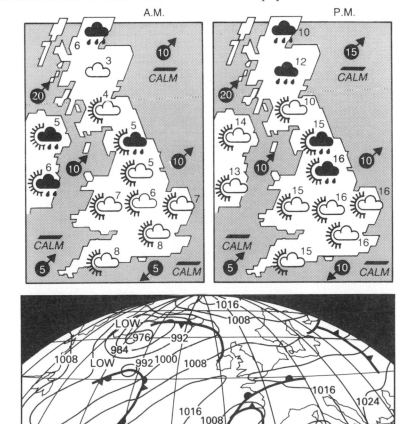

The Times: 5 May 1988
(information supplied by the Meteorological Office)

15

From newspapers for July 1987 they obtained the data given below:

July 1987		Bournemouth				Torquay			
		Sun (h)	Max °C	°F		Sun (h)	Max °C	°F	
Wed	1	10.1	23	73	sunny	10.0	22	72	sunny
Thurs	2	10.6	20	70	sunny	7.8	19	66	sunny
Fri	3	13.3	22	72	sunny	13.7	19	66	sunny
Sat	4	14.1	21	70	sunny	14.5	20	68	sunny
Mon	6	15.4	27	81	sunny	15.1	24	75	sunny
Tues	7	11.8	25	77	sunny	12.3	26	79	sunny
Wed	8	11.0	26	79	sunny	11.5	25	77	sunny
Thurs	9	13.6	26	79	sunny	11.5	22	72	sunny
Fri	10	13.1	22	72	sunny	8.8	19	66	sunny
Sat	11	6.9	22	72	sunny	–	–	–	–
Mon	13	8.7	23	73	bright	6.9	22	72	bright
Tues	14	14.0	23	73	sunny	13.5	22	72	sunny
Wed	15	1.6	20	68	shower	0.7	19	66	rain
Fri	17	8.0	20	68	sunny	7.8	20	68	shower
Sat	18	2.6	18	64	shower	2.3	12	63	shower
Mon	20	0.5	17	63	rain	1.6	20	68	bright
Tues	21	2.7	19	66	bright	3.8	20	68	bright
Wed	22	–	16	61	shower	2.2	20	68	cloudy
Thurs	23	0.2	18	64	drizzle	0.5	19	66	cloudy
Fri	24	0.2	18	64	cloudy	2.0	19	66	bright
Sat	25	–	20	68	dull	3.0	22	72	cloudy
Mon	27	8.7	21	70	sunny	5.5	19	66	bright
Tues	28	2.8	21	70	bright	4.6	22	72	bright
Wed	29	3.2	22	72	cloudy	5.1	23	73	sunny
Thurs	30	3.9	22	72	shower	5.1	21	70	bright
Fri	31	4.4	21	70	bright	7.6	19	66	bright

A simple pictorial representation of the temperatures (°C) for Bournemouth might be a bar chart.

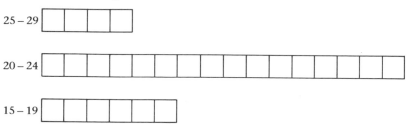

A **stem and leaf diagram** (or **stem plot**) is similar to this but has the advantage of retaining all the detail of the original data.

Stem (tens)	Leaf (units)
2	5 6 6 7
2	0 0 0 0 1 1 1 1 2 2 2 2 2 3 3 3
1	6 7 8 8 8 9

key 1|6 means 16°C

> Stem and leaf diagrams always use equal class intervals.

The previous example used class intervals of 5°C and the leaves were arranged in numerical order.

Draw a stem and leaf diagram for the data for Bournemouth using intervals of 10°C, i.e. 10–19, 20–29.
Also draw diagrams using intervals of 1°C and of 2°C.
Which diagram do you think gives the best pictorial representation of the data?

Stem and leaf diagrams can be used to compare two samples by showing the results together on a 'back-to-back' stem plot. In the following example, the twenty-six temperatures for Bournemouth are compared with the twenty-five temperatures for Torquay.

Daily maximum temperatures for July 1987

Bournemouth   Torquay

```
              7  6  6 | 2 | 6
                    5 | 2 | 4  5
  3  3  3  2  2  2  2  2 | 2 | 2  2  2  2  2  3
     1  1  1  1  0  0  0  0 | 2 | 0  0  0  0  0  1
              9  8  8  8 | 1 | 9  9  9  9  9  9  9  9
                    7  6 | 1 |
                         | 1 |
                         | 1 | 2
```

5|2 means 25°C   1|9 means 19°C

> From this back-to-back stem plot, what would you deduce about the relative temperatures of Bournemouth and Torquay?

Stem and leaf diagrams provide a quick visual display of data. Consider the following diagram comparing two different experimental methods of measuring the speed of a bullet. Twenty readings were taken for each of methods A and B.

Method A								Method B				
						6	51	0	2			
							50	1	3	3	8	
		8	7	3	3	1	49	0	5	5	7	8
9	7	7	5	2	1	1	0	48	1	2	2	6	9
		8	5	5	1	1	47	0	4	8		
						4	46	3				

$8 \mid 47$ means $478\,\text{ms}^{-1}$ $49 \mid 5$ means $495\,\text{ms}^{-1}$

> What impression of the data can be obtained from stem and leaf plots?

The stem plot gives an impression of:
- the average;
- the variability

of the data.

A deeper analysis than that afforded by the purely pictorial stem plot can follow, once overall patterns have been spotted. Some further practice in using stem plots to obtain impressions about data is given on the following tasksheet.

 TASKSHEET 1 — Stem and leaf (page 31)

The stem plot gives an impression of whether or not the data are symmetric and/or unimodal.

EXERCISE 1

1   Draw a back-to-back stem plot for the hours of sunshine at Bournemouth and Torquay during July 1987. What conclusions can you draw from this pictorial representation of the data?

2   Use a stem plot to compare the examination marks of two classes.

Class 1   80 62 53 76 76 31 59 78 84
66 71 50 79 69 87 64 56 65
58 78 75 60 51

Class 2   71 68 56 79 73 51 48 83 64
58 75 45 91 80 59 34 55 73
81 62 64 69

(a)   Which class has performed better in the examination?

(b)   Which class appears to be less variable in terms of pupil ability?

3   The following (in thousands of pounds) are starting salaries for graduates in 'sales' and 'technical' jobs.

15, 11, 9, 12, 7.5, 8, 10, 16, 11, 12, 10, 9, 10, 14, 9.5, 13, 8.5, 8, 8.5, 12, 11, 9, 11, 7, 10, 13.

Draw a stem plot for the data. Comment on its shape. Is it what you would have expected?

2.3 Numerical representation of data

Sometimes it is important to condense a large data set into a few numbers which give an impression of the original set. Consider the following example:

Ice dance scores

```
5 | 1
5 | 2  2  2
5 | 3  3
5 | 4  4
5 | 5
```

5|2 means 5.2

Judges' scores

5.1	5.3	5.2	5.3	5.4	5.4	5.2	5.5	5.2

For such a data set, besides a pictorial representation it is also often useful to have a single number (an 'average') which best **represents** the data.

> Give reasons why each of the following numbers could be said to *represent* the data set above:
>
> 5.2, 5.3, 5.29.

Reminder

The **mode** is the **most frequently** occurring value.

The **median** is the **middle value** when the data are ranked in decreasing (or increasing) order of magnitude.

The **mean** is the sum of the data values divided by the number of observations.

TASKSHEET 2 — Representative numbers for the average (page 32)

The three commonly used 'averages' are each appropriate in different circumstances and for different purposes.

What properties do you think that a number should have if it is to be used to represent a set?

Describe situations where the most appropriate average would be

(a) the mode;

(b) the mean;

(c) the median.

EXERCISE 2

1 Fifty people who entered a raffle were asked afterwards how many winning tickets they had bought. Forty-one had none, six had one and three had two.

Calculate the mean, median and mode of the number of winning tickets per person.

Which is the most suitable measure of the average in this case?

2 In an aptitude test, twenty people were asked to do a jigsaw puzzle and the time taken by each was recorded, with the following results:

	13	34	40	43
	45	46	48	49
Time (seconds)	51	52	52	53
	58	63	72	75
	76	78	104	

As can be seen, only nineteen people completed the jigsaw.

(a) Calculate the mean and median of these data and decide which you think is the most appropriate measure of average, giving your reasons.

(b) The twentieth person gave up after 148 seconds. Should this information have been included in your calculations? Give reasons for your answer, stating how the observation would affect the mean and the median.

3 The distribution of the ages of the inhabitants of a south coast seaside town has the following shape:

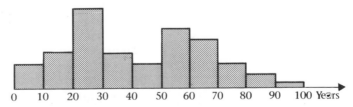

Comment on the shape of the distribution and how you might measure the average age for the inhabitants of this town.

2.4 Box and whisker diagrams

A **box plot** or **box and whisker diagram** is a pictorial representation of data based upon five numbers: top of range, upper quartile, median, lower quartile and bottom of range. These are illustrated in the box plot of reaction times (in hundredths of a second) shown below.

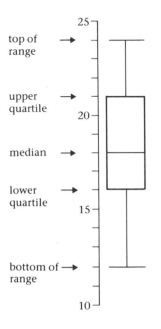

A quarter of the values lie between 12 and 16, a quarter between 16 and 18, a quarter between 18 and 21 and a quarter between 21 and 24 (hundredths of a second).

The middle 50% of the data lies within the box. The length of the box (the **interquartile range**) is a measure of the variability or spread of the data.

The box plot for a perfectly symmetric distribution would look something like the one drawn below:

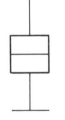

The whiskers are of equal length.

The median is in the middle of the box.

If the distribution had most of its values at the lower end of the range the box plot might be as shown in the diagram:

> Describe some of the features of the box plot above.

As an example of how box plots can be used, consider the following. To ensure consistency of marking, an examinations board employs a senior examiner to check a sample of each examiner's scripts. A list of the resulting alterations forms a data set which needs analysing.

Box plots for the alterations of marks for samples of two examiners' scripts are shown.

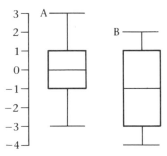

From the box plot, you can see that 50% of the scripts marked by A required a change in mark of at most one mark.

Use the box plots shown above to compare and comment on the marking of the two examiners.

Which examiner was the more lenient?
Which was the more reliable?

EXERCISE 3

1 Box plots for the experimental data on the speed of a bullet are as shown.

What can be deduced from the box plots alone?

Bullet speeds in m s^{-1}

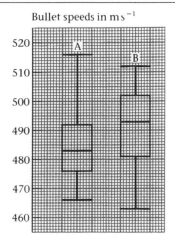

23

2   Box plots for the maximum daily temperatures during one month, for London and Copenhagen, are as shown.

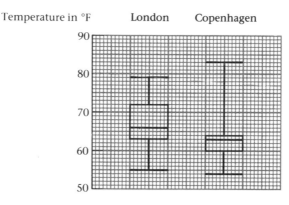

(a) Which city had the highest recorded temperature? Which city was generally hotter? Carefully justify your answer.

(b) Which city had the greater range of temperature? Which city would you consider to have had the more variable temperature? Carefully justify your answer.

3   Box plots for the alterations in marks for samples of scripts from each member of a team of examiners are as shown.

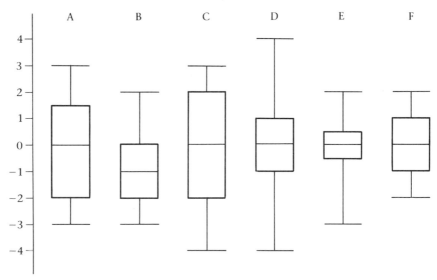

(a) Which examiner is the most reliable marker? Justify your answer.

(b) The examination board only requires a team of five for the following year's examinations. Which examiner would you drop from the team? Give reasons for your answer.

(c) What would you advise the board to do with the other scripts marked by examiner B? (Other than re-marking all of them!)

2.5 Constructing box plots

Medical statistics are used for purposes as varied as deciding between alternative treatments, determining appropriate premiums for medical insurance schemes and estimating future medical provision.

Length of stay (days)	No. of males	No. of females
0	6	4
1	15	2
2	4	3
3	2	4
4	5	2
5	8	1
6	16	4
7	12	2
8	9	5
9	11	5
10	10	0
11	18	0
12	7	2
13	2	3
14	5	2
15	7	0
16	1	2
17	3	0
18	1	1
19	1	0
21	1	0
22	2	1
23	0	1
24	1	1
26	1	0
28	1	1
29	0	2
37	2	0
41	1	0
45	0	1
72	0	1
Totals	152	50

This table, which shows the lengths of stay in hospital following a myocardial infarction (heart attack), was provided by St Thomas' Hospital, London, from their Hospital Activity Analysis database for 1986 admissions.

Why would a stem plot be inappropriate for these data?

A cumulative frequency diagram can be used to represent such data pictorially.

TASKSHEET   3S   —   Cumulative frequency diagrams (page 34)

The number of patients staying **up to** a certain number of days in hospital is plotted against the length of stay in days.

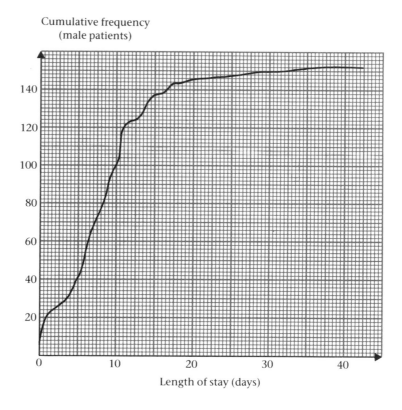

Cumulative frequency (male patients)

Length of stay (days)

> Obtain from the graph the median and the quartiles for the length of stay for male patients.

It is possible, indeed it is often quicker, to estimate the median and quartiles directly from the original data.

The middle length of stay for males was between the lengths of stay for the 76th and 77th patients, both of whom stayed 8 days.

The median was 8 days for males.

There were 76 patients who stayed less than 8 days. The middle length of stay for these was between the lengths of stay for the 38th and 39th patients, both of whom stayed 5 days.

The lower quartile can be thought of as the median of the data items **below** the median.

The lower quartile was 5 days for males.

> Find the upper quartile using this technique.

The box plot for length of stay for males is:

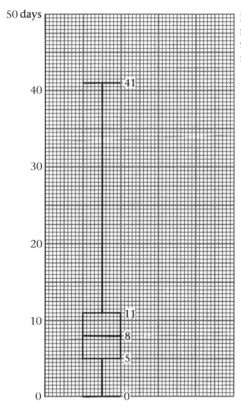

Length of stay for male patients following myocardial infarction

> Obtain the equivalent box plot for females. Draw the two box plots on the same scale and use them to compare the lengths of stay for male and female patients. Comment also on the shapes of the two distributions based on the evidence of the box plots.

From a stem plot with the results already written in numerical order it is easy to extract the values of the median and quartiles, although it is important to note carefully the **direction** in which the numbers follow on. It may help to imagine the data written out on a line.

Consider the following back-to-back stem plot for data obtained during an experiment on reaction times.

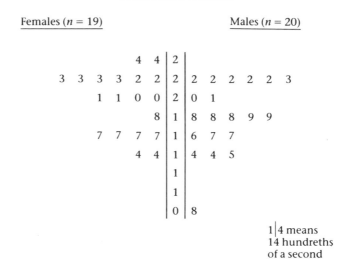

Adult reaction times

Females (*n* = 19)   Males (*n* = 20)

1|4 means
14 hundreths
of a second

Median There are 20 reaction times for males. The two middle values are the 10th and 11th (18 and 19 hundredths of a second) and so the median is 0.185 seconds.

Lower quartile There are 10 values below the median. The middle values are the 5th and 6th (16 and 17 hundredths of a second) and so the lower quartile is 0.165 seconds.

Find the median for females and the remaining quartiles for both sets of reaction times given above.

EXERCISE 4

1 Draw box plots for the male and female reaction times given above. What conclusions can you draw from them?

2 Draw box plots for the data of question 2 of exercise 1. Describe how they confirm the general conclusions made from the original stem plots.

3 Use box plots for 1978 and 1985 to draw some conclusions about any changes in total alcohol consumption.

| | Alcohol Consumption Litres per head of 100% alcohol | | |
	1978	1985	% change
France	16.3	13.9	−15
East Germany	11.5	13.4	+17
Portugal	9.9	13.1	+32
Hungary	12.2	12.3	+0.8
Spain	14.3	11.8	−17.5
West Germany	12.9	11.3	−12.5
Austria	10.4	11.1	+6.7
Belgium	10.2	10.8	+5.8
Switzerland	10.4	10.8	+3.8
Czechoslavakia	11.6	9.9	−14.7
Denmark	8.9	9.8	+10.0
Italy	12.0	9.4	−21.7
Australia	9.8	9.2	−6.2
Argentina	11.2	8.7	−22.4
Bulgaria	9.2	8.7	−5.7
Netherlands	8.9	8.4	−5.9
New Zealand	8.5	8.1	−4.8
Canada	8.4	7.8	−7.7
USA	8.2	7.7	−6.1
UK	7.2	7.1	−1.4
Eire	7.7	6.9	−10.4
Greece	6.1	6.8	+11.4
Poland	8.3	6.7	−23.8
Finland	6.3	5.9	−6.4
USSR	6.2	5.7	−8.1
Yugoslavia	7.8	5.3	−32.1
Sweden	5.9	4.8	−18.7
Japan	5.6	4.4	−21.5
Norway	4.0	4.1	+2.5

Brewers' Society Statistical Handbook 1986
The Sunday Times: 26 June 1988

4 The back-to-back stem plot drawn below gives the daily hours of sunshine measured at the Weston Park Meteorological Station in Sheffield.

```
              January                        July

                                   |13| 6
                                   |12| 0
                                   |11| 1  5
                                   |10| 1
                                   | 9| 7
                                   | 8|
                                   | 7| 0  3  6  7  9
                            2      | 6| 2  6
                        8   7      | 5| 5  6  7  8  8
                                   | 4| 3  8  8
                        3   0      | 3| 1  3
                    4   3   1      | 2| 5  6
                    9   7   5      | 1| 6
8  7  5  5  4  3  1  0  0  0  0  0  0  0  0  0  0  0  0  0  0| 0| 0  0  1  6  8
```

6|2 means 6.2 hours

(a) What conclusions can you draw directly from the stem plot?

(b) For each month, find

   (i) the median;

   (ii) the lower quartile;

   (iii) the upper quartile.

(c) Using a common scale, draw box plots for the daily hours of sunshine for January and July.

(d) What are your conclusions from the box plots?

After working through this chapter you should:

1 be able to construct stem and leaf plots from data and use these plots to indicate central tendency, variability and symmetry of the data;

2 be able to construct box and whiskers plots from raw data, cumulative frequency diagrams and stem and leaf plots;

3 be able to use box and whiskers plots to indicate the median, quartiles, range, variability and symmetry of a data set;

4 be able to choose an appropriate average, mode, mean or median, for a given data set;

5 understand the terms symmetric, skewed, unimodal and bimodal as applied to distributions.

Stem and leaf

The table gives the heights (in cm) of twenty married couples.

Wife	Husband
159	180
162	165
142	161
159	173
158	174
139	173
170	173
155	179
156	184
154	177
159	178
163	175
158	168
161	171
152	171
171	175
143	173
158	182
164	164
156	174

1 By considering the data in the table, say which of the two heights is more variable.

2 (a) Draw stem and leaf plots for the heights of the husbands and wives separately.

  (b) Which set of heights is more variable?

  (c) Which has the higher middle value?

  (d) Find the median in each case.

3 Consider the data as a set of the heights of 40 adults and draw a 'combined' stem and leaf plot. Comment on its shape.

4 If the group of adults is representative of the population, which of the distributions below is most likely to represent that of adults' height? Explain your choice.

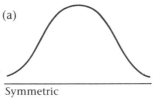

(a)

Symmetric
One mode (unimodal)

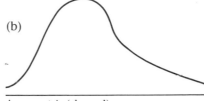

(b)

Asymmetric (skewed)
Unimodal

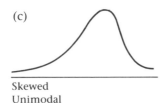

(c)

Skewed
Unimodal

(d)

Two modes (bimodal)

A unimodal distribution which is not symmetric is said to be **skewed**.

Representative numbers for the average

1 You will be familiar with the mean, median and the mode. Complete the following for the family sizes shown above.

    Mean   =

    Mode   =

    Median =

In what way can each of these be thought of as representing the 'average' family?

There are two interesting ways of obtaining 'averages' by minimising certain functions. These involve the idea of **absolute value**, which you may have met as the function ABS in using a calculator or computer. An alternative name for the function is the **modulus.**

The modulus of any real number a, written $|a|$, is defined as follows:

$$|a| = \begin{cases} a \text{ if } a \geq 0, \\ -a \text{ if } a < 0. \end{cases}$$

For example:

    $|2.5| = 2.5$, $|-3| = 3$.

You will see that the expression $|a - b|$ represents the (unsigned) **distance between** a and b on the number line. For example, consider this table of values for $|x - 4|$:

x	...	−1	0	1	2	3	4	5	...
$|x - 4|$	...	5	4	3	2	1	0	1	...

The size of each of the families in question 1 can be represented on the number line as shown below.

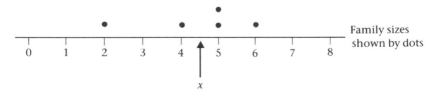

You wish to find a number x somewhere on the line as a representative number for family size. The question to consider is where to place x. To make the marked points cluster around x as closely as possible, you might try minimising the sum of all the distances of the points from x.

2 Using a graphic calculator or computer, plot the graph of

$$y = |x - 2| + |x - 4| + |x - 5| + |x - 5| + |x - 6|$$

for values of x from 0 to 8.

For what value of x is y a minimum?

What is the median value for the data set 2, 4, 5, 5, 6?

3 (a) Consider the data set 1, 3, 5.

    (i) What is the median value?

    (ii) Plot the graph of $y = |x - 1| + |x - 3| + |x - 5|$. What value of x makes y a minimum?

  (b) Investigate other small data sets and make notes on your findings.

Instead of minimising a sum of distances you might try minimising a sum of **squares of distances**.

4 (a) Consider the data set 1, 2, 5.

    (i) Plot the graph of

$$y = (x - 1)^2 + (x - 2)^2 + (x - 5)^2$$

    What is the value of x at the minimum point?

    (ii) What statistical measure of the data set have you obtained?

  (b) Investigate other small data sets and make a note of your observations.

Cumulative frequency diagrams

TASKSHEET **3S**

The **cumulative frequency** is the total frequency up to a particular value, or class boundary.

340 sunflower plants were measured six weeks after planting. From the frequency table it is easy to draw up a cumulative frequency table as shown.

Height (cm)	Frequency
3–6	10
7–10	21
11–14	114
15–18	105
19–22	54
23–26	36

Height (cm)	Cumulative frequency
up to 6.5	10
up to 10.5	10 + 21 = 31
up to 14.5	31 + 114 = 145
up to 18.5	145 + 105 = 250
up to 22.5	250 + 54 = 304
up to 26.5	304 + 36 = 340

It can be helpful to plot cumulative frequencies on a cumulative frequency diagram or **ogive**.

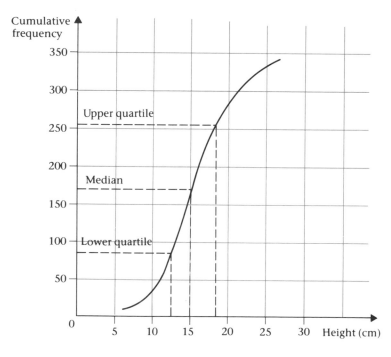

Using the cumulative frequency diagram, the median can be estimated quite easily. For 340 plants, the median (or middle plant) will be approximately the 170th plant. By finding 170 on the cumulative frequency axis you can read off the corresponding height on the horizontal axis. The median height is 15 cm.

The lower quartile can be found by reading off the height for the 85th plant. The upper quartile can be found by reading off the height of the 255th plant.

1 Find the values of the lower and upper quartiles.

2 A gardener collected 150 worms from her garden and recorded their lengths to the nearest millimetre. The results are given below.

Length (mm)	95–109	110–124	125–139	140–154	155–169	170–184	185–199	200–214
No. of worms	4	10	19	36	43	26	9	3

   (a) Write down the cumulative frequency table and draw a cumulative frequency curve to illustrate this information.

   (b) Use the curve to estimate the median and interquartile range.

   (c) What percentage of worms are less than 150 mm in length?

3 Data analysis revisited

3.1 Introduction

A census of the
United Kingdom
population is taken
every 10 years.
The idea of counting
and collecting information
or data has a long
history:

. . . as the Lord had commanded Moses. He drew up the lists . . .
in the wilderness of Sinai. The total number of Israelites aged
20 years and upwards fit for service, recorded in the lists of
fathers' families, was 603 550.

Numbers 1:19, 45–46

Today the collection and analysis of census data is undertaken by a
special government department – The Office of Population, Census
and Surveys. The questions asked on the census form are sometimes
the cause of considerable national debate, for example, whether or
not to include questions on the ethnic background of householders.

> Give some reasons why a census was thought to be important
> historically and why it is important today. To what uses can
> census data be put?

Some information from a census is provided on datasheet 1.

DATASHEET 1 – *Living conditions (Teacher's resource file)*

> Draw a stem and leaf diagram for the data about the
> metropolitan districts. Comment on the suitability of a stem and
> leaf diagram for this data.

3.2 Grouping data

When dealing with large amounts of data, it is often much more convenient and sensible to collect the data values in groups. A possible grouping for the census data from the non-metropolitan counties is given below.

Number of substandard households (per 1000) in the non-metropolitan counties

Number of households (per 1000)	Frequency
60–79	2
80–99	2
100–119	5
120–139	7
140–159	9
160–179	7
180–199	4
200–219	1
220–239	2

Notice that here the groups are of equal width (60–79, 80–99 etc.) but often this is not the case. If there are few values in a group then several groups can be combined. For example, the data on substandard households could be re-grouped as follows:

No. of households (per 1000)	Frequency		No. of households (per 1000)	Frequency
60–99	4	*or*	60–139	16
100–119	5		140–179	16
120–139	7		180–239	7
140–159	9			
160–179	7			
180–239	7			

What should you consider when deciding what group widths to use?

Group the data on the metropolitan districts from datasheet 1 into a grouping of your choice.

3.3 Representing grouped data – histograms

The lengths of 20 screws were measured. The results are shown below in a frequency table, together with a diagram to illustrate the data.

Length (mm)	Frequency
0–20	5
20–25	5
25–30	8
30–35	2

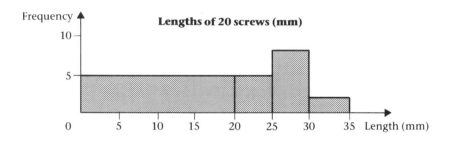

Does the diagram provide a good representation of the data?

Justify your answer.

Consider a further data set. The frequency distribution shown is for the length of each of 250 rods.

Length (mm)	5–7.5	7.5–10	10–12.5	12.5–15	15–17.5	17.5–20	20–22.5	22.5–25	25–27.5	27.5–30
Frequency	4	1	0	10	60	84	58	20	12	1

Draw a frequency diagram for the data as presented.
Re-group the data into the intervals: 5–15, 15–17.5, 17.5–20, 20–22.5, 22.5–30 and redraw the diagram.

Comment on whether this sort of diagram provides a good representation of the data.

Representing the frequency by the height of the block causes problems when the data are grouped into **unequal group intervals**. It is the actual size or **area** of the block which is needed to represent the frequency.

frequency = area of block = width of interval × height of block

$$\text{height of block} = \frac{\text{frequency}}{\text{width of interval}} = \text{frequency density}$$

Applying this idea to the distribution of screw lengths, the following frequency densities are obtained:

Length (mm)	Interval width	Frequency	Frequency density
0–20	20	5	$\frac{5}{20} = 0.25$
20–25	5	5	$\frac{5}{5} = 1.00$
25–30	5	8	$\frac{8}{5} = 1.60$
30–35	5	2	$\frac{2}{5} = 0.40$

The diagram is as follows:

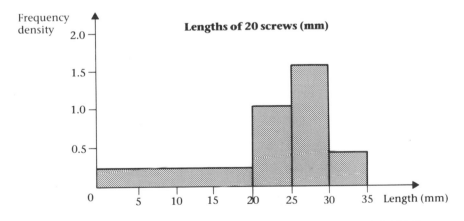

Which type of diagram best illustrates the distribution? Explain why.

A frequency diagram where the frequency is represented by area is called a **histogram.** Note that there are **no gaps** between the groups and the vertical axis represents frequency density, **not** frequency.

3.4 Problems with data

When handling quantitative data you need to be conscious of the existence of two distinct types of data – **continuous** and **discrete**.

Continuous data can, theoretically, be **any** values within a continuous range. Discrete data can only take certain values within a range. Examples of measurements which would produce continuous data are height, weight, and time. Examples of discrete measurements are marks on a test (0, 1, 2, . . .) or numbers in a family (1, 2, 3, . . .). In practice, measurements of length or weight may be given to the nearest metre or kilogram, so recorded measurements are always discrete data.

It is always important to consider the nature of the data, especially when drawing histograms. In the last section you saw how to draw a histogram for continuous measurements. The example shows how to handle discrete data and also illustrates how to deal with the common problem of a group for which the interval is not fully defined.

EXAMPLE 1

In a traffic survey, the number of cars passing a point in a one-minute interval was recorded over 120 successive intervals. The results were as follows:

Number of cars (N)	0–9	10–14	15–19	20–29	30+
Frequency (f)	18	46	35	13	8

Draw a histogram for this data.

SOLUTION

To avoid gaps in the histogram the intervals are re-defined in a convenient way. This is illustrated in the sketch below for the 10–14 range (possible values 10, 11, 12, 13 and 14 only).

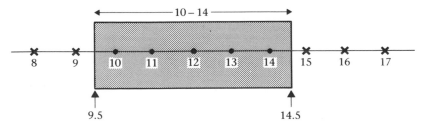

The first interval would therefore be re-defined as −0.5–9.5 to include all the ten discrete data values from 0 to 9.

The frequency table becomes:

Class interval	−0.5–9.5	9.5–14.5	14.5–19.5	19.5–29.5	29.5–49.5
Frequency	18	46	35	13	8
Frequency density	$\frac{18}{10} = 1.80$	$\frac{46}{5} = 9.20$	$\frac{35}{5} = 7.00$	$\frac{13}{10} = 1.30$	$\frac{8}{20} = 0.40$

Notice that the last group (30+) has been defined to be of width 20, twice the width of the 20–29 group.

Under what circumstances would this decision be reasonable?

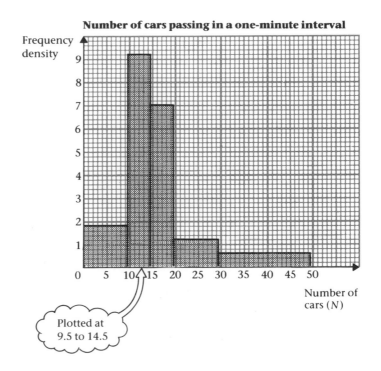

Number of cars passing in a one-minute interval

Frequency density

Number of cars (N)

Plotted at 9.5 to 14.5

EXERCISE 1

1

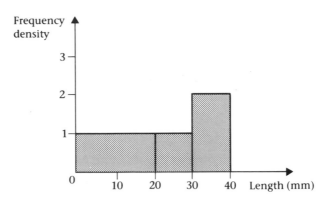

For the histogram shown

(a) how many of the lengths are in the intervals

    (i) 20–30 mm   (ii) 30–40 mm   (iii) 0–20 mm?

(b) what is the total frequency?

2 For the histogram shown, find the total frequency.

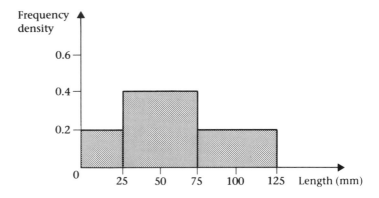

3 Construct histograms for the following data sets.

(a)

Volume (cm^3)	f
0–5	5
5–10	5
10–20	10
20–30	20
30–40	10
40–60	5

(b)

Number of cars per hour	f
50–59	10
60–79	30
80–99	20
100–139	10

4 Rainfall data is provided below for 50 weather stations in the north of England and 50 in the south. Each figure represents total rainfall (in mm) for June 1987.

(a) Decide on a sensible grouping, which should be the same for the north and south. (Consider using unequal widths if this is sensible.)

(b) Construct frequency tables based on your choice of group size.

(c) Draw histograms for both data sets separately.

(d) Comment briefly on the two distributions.

Northern weather stations (mm of rain)

59	106	109	74	104	115	94	225	140	217
146	149	140	121	132	78	114	86	87	126
120	101	125	108	105	112	97	83	77	88
106	123	95	113	105	144	117	107	174	176
108	87	110	95	78	103	87	83	87	80

Southern weather stations (mm of rain)

89	89	111	93	73	121	103	80	108	88
75	79	103	107	70	82	97	59	90	53
67	46	43	65	112	115	99	217	83	61
98	90	95	87	86	77	96	70	111	74
81	70	72	87	68	85	100	67	54	109

5 Draw histograms to represent the data on substandard housing in the non-metropolitan counties and metropolitan districts on datasheet 1. (Use the same grouping for both histograms.) Comment briefly on the two distributions.

3.5 Averages and spread

You have seen that the mean, median and mode are all measures of the 'average' value of a set of data. The mean is particularly important in statistical work and a special symbol ($\bar{x}$) is introduced for it.

Suppose the observed values are $x_1, x_2, x_3, \ldots, x_r, \ldots, x_n$.

$$\text{Mean} = \frac{\text{Sum of observed values}}{\text{Number of observations}}$$

x bar – for the mean of the values

$$\bar{x} = \frac{\text{Sum}(x_1, x_2, \ldots, x_n)}{n}$$

$$\bar{x} = \frac{1}{n}\sum x$$

Sigma *x* – for the sum of the observations

Keys for $\boxed{\bar{x}}$ and $\boxed{\sum x}$ are on your calculator.

> Check that you can use your calculator to obtain $\sum x$ and $\bar{x}$ for a set of values.

The following are the scores awarded to two gymnasts in a competition:

First gymnast	9.7	9.8	9.7	9.8	9.8	9.7
Second gymnast	8.8	9.2	8.8	9.8	9.4	9.8

The scores can be shown along a number line as follows:

First gymnast

Second gymnast

The scores of the second gymnast are much more spread out. It is useful to have a **number to represent spread**: for this you need to define a reference point and consider how spread out the observations are about the reference point.

> What might be a sensible reference point? Define a measure of spread about this point.

It is conventional to take the mean as the reference point. One measure of spread considers the mean of the deviations from the mean. This is the mean absolute deviation. A second and more important measure takes the **mean of the squared distances from the mean**. This is the **variance**.

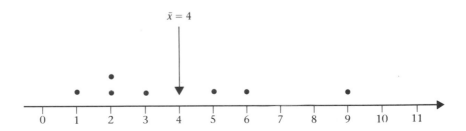

$\bar{x} = 4$

> Confirm that, for this set of values, $\bar{x} = 4$ and the total of the square distances from the mean is 48.

There are 7 data values. The mean of the squared distances of each value from the mean is $\frac{48}{7} = 6.86$.

Variance = 6.86

> Find the mean and variance of the scores for each gymnast.

Statisticians use the variance and the **square root of the variance**, called the **standard deviation**, to measure spread. Both are in common use.

> The mean of the sum of the squared distances from the mean is called the **variance**. It is conventional to use the square root of the variance as a measure of spread around the mean. This is called the **standard deviation**.
>
> **standard deviation** $= \sqrt{\text{variance}}$

TASKSHEET 1 — Standard deviation and variance (page 54)

You should have observed the following results for the mean and standard deviation.

> When all data values are multiplied by a constant a, then the new mean and standard deviation are both a times the original mean and standard deviation.
>
> When a constant value b, is added to all data values, then the mean is also increased by b. However, the standard deviation does not change.

The phrase 'standard deviation' is often abbreviated to S.D. and the symbol used to denote standard deviation is, by convention, the letter s. The result above can then be expressed as

Original data values	x_1	$x_2 \ldots$	x_n	mean $=$	$\bar{x}$;	S.D. $= s$
Data values if multiplied by a	ax_1	$ax_2 \ldots$	ax_n	mean $=$	$a\bar{x}$;	S.D. $= as$
Data values if b is added	$x_1 + b$	$x_2 + b \ldots$	$x_n + b$	mean $= \bar{x} + b$;		S.D. $= s$

EXERCISE 2

1 A student measures the resistance of a piece of wire, repeating the experiment six times to check her results. Her results are:

Resistance (ohms)	54.2	53.7	55.0	53.7	54.0	54.6

(a) Find the mean and standard deviation of the readings.

(b) She discovers that each reading in the table is 10% too high, because of faulty equipment. Write down the new mean and standard deviation.

2 A teacher has 32 pupils in the class, having a mean age of 14 years and a standard deviation of 0.25 years. Write down the standard deviation of the ages of the same 32 pupils two years later.

3 The temperature is recorded at 12 weather stations in and around London on a given day. The mean recorded temperature is 12°C, with a standard deviation of 0.5°C. Write down the mean temperature and the standard deviation in degrees Fahrenheit.

3.6 A formula for variance and standard deviation

Sometimes it is necessary to have a formula for the variance. This is important not simply in **calculating** a variance but it can also be useful in general mathematical work, for example to see how the variance relates to other measures. You can obtain a formula as follows:

Suppose a set of data values is $x_1, x_2, x_3, \ldots, x_n$, having a mean value of $\bar{x}$.

The squared distances from the mean are:

$(x_1 - \bar{x})^2, (x_2 - \bar{x})^2, \ldots, (x_n - \bar{x})^2$

The total of these squared distances is $\sum (x - \bar{x})^2$.

> This means add up all the squared distances $(x - \bar{x})^2$

So the mean of the squared distance is $\dfrac{\sum (x - \bar{x})^2}{n}$.

$$\text{Variance} = \frac{\sum (x - \bar{x})^2}{n}.$$

$$\text{Standard deviation} = \sqrt{\frac{\sum (x - \bar{x})^2}{n}}.$$

In practice it is often difficult to use this result and an alternative expression is sometimes more useful.

TASKSHEET 2 — Variance by direct calculation (page 55)

An alternative expression for the variance is

$$\frac{\sum x^2}{n} - \bar{x}^2$$

3.7 Variance for frequency distributions

In a frequency distribution there may be many different occurrences of the same value. A simple example would be the data set:

14.3, 14.4, 14.5, 14.4, 14.4.

Observation	Frequency
14.3	1
14.4	3
14.5	1

> Calculate the mean and variance of this data set.

If a data value x_1 occurs, say f_1 times, then the term $(x_1 - \bar{x})^2$ will need to be added into the total squared deviation f_1 times.

i.e. total squared deviation for the f_1 data values $= (x_1 - \bar{x})^2 \times f_1$

> Show that for a frequency distribution
>
> $$\bar{x} = \frac{\sum xf}{\sum f} \;,\; \text{variance} = \frac{\sum (x - \bar{x})^2 f}{\sum f}$$

It is clear that, with increasingly large data sets and frequency distributions, the calculations will become very tedious. Fortunately, as the variance (and standard deviation) are so important, calculators with statistical functions can obtain the required values easily, provided that the data is entered correctly.

> Find out how to use your calculator to obtain means, variances and standard deviations.

3.8 The mean and variance for grouped data

The table shows the number of shots played in each of fifty rallies between two tennis players before and after a coaching session. Only the grouped data for the length of each of the fifty rallies are recorded, not the original results.

	Number of rallies	
Number of shots in rally	Before coaching	After coaching
1–10	32	5
11–20	12	20
21–30	3	15
31–40	2	3
41–50	1	5
51–60	–	2
Total	50	50

Use the mid-interval value as representative of the length of rally in the group. The 'before coaching' table becomes:

Before coaching

Group	Midpoint	Frequency
1–10	5.5	32
11–20	15.5	12
21–30	25.5	3
31–40	35.5	2
41–50	$\frac{41+50}{2} = 45.5$ → 45.5	1

Take each of the rallies in the 1–10 group as having 5.5 shots. The total number of shots played for these 32 rallies is **estimated** to be $32 \times 5.5 = 176$.

The data can now be entered into your calculator as:

32 rallies of 5.5,
12 rallies of 15.5, etc.

49

Enter the data in your calculator and confirm that the values of the mean rally length and the standard deviation are 11.1 and 9.2 respectively.

For direct calculations, the formula for the variance for grouped frequency distributions would be obtained as follows.

Let the group mid-value be x. Let the number of data values be f.

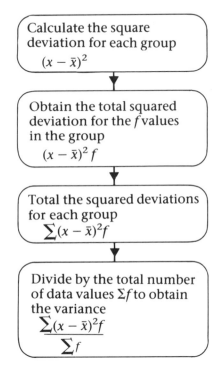

Calculate the square deviation for each group
$$(x - \bar{x})^2$$

Obtain the total squared deviation for the f values in the group
$$(x - \bar{x})^2 f$$

Total the squared deviations for each group
$$\sum (x - \bar{x})^2 f$$

Divide by the total number of data values $\sum f$ to obtain the variance
$$\frac{\sum (x - \bar{x})^2 f}{\sum f}$$

$$\text{Variance} = \frac{\sum (x - \bar{x})^2 f}{\sum f}$$

An alternative form, which is more useful in calculations and often more accurate, is:

$$\text{Variance} = \frac{\sum x^2 f}{\sum f} - \bar{x}^2$$

EXERCISE 3

You should use the statistical functions on your calculator for this exercise.

1 (a) Calculate the mean and standard deviation of the length of rallies 'after coaching'.

(b) Has the coaching made a difference in this case? Justify your answer.

2 The projected population distribution of England and Wales for the year 2025 is given below. Calculate

(a) the total population;

(b) the mean and standard deviation of the age of the population.

Be careful with age calculations!

This group has people from 15 to **just** below 30.

The midpoint will be

$$\frac{15 + 30}{2} = 22.5 \text{ yrs.}$$

Age group (years)	Frequency (thousands)
0–14	9928
15–29	9953
30–44	10075
45–59	9808
60–74	8989
75–89	4289
90–99	469

3 The age distribution of the population of England and Wales in 1986 is given below.

Age group (years)	Mid-value x (years)	Frequency (thousands)
0–14	7.5	9410
15–29	22.5	11835
30–44	37.5	10202
45–59	52.5	8147
60–74	67.5	7171
75–89	82.5	3114
90+	95	184

> Take the group for 90+ to be 90–99 years old.

(a) Why is it reasonable to take the last group to be 90–99 years?

(b) Calculate the mean and standard deviation of the population in 1986.

(c) Using your answers to questions 2 and 3(b), comment on what is expected to happen to the age distribution in England and Wales as the years pass.

4 Information on the amount of mortgage taken out by house buyers in January 1987 is given in the table.

Mortgages for various types of house buyer (1987)

Amount	All buyers (%)	First-time buyers (%)	Other buyers (%)
Under £10000	6	6	6
£10000–£13999	9	11	7
£14000–£17999	12	15	10
£18000–£21999	13	15	12
£22000–£24999	9	10	8
£25000–£29999	15	15	16
£30000+	36	28	41

(a) Choose what you consider to be a sensible upper value for the last group.

(b) Find the mean and standard deviation of the loans taken by first-time buyers and other buyers.

(c) Comment on your results.

After working through this chapter you should:

1   be able to draw histograms for discrete and continuous data;

2   know that the mean is often taken as the reference point for spread;

3   know that the variance is the mean of the total of all the squared deviations from the mean;

4   know that the standard deviation is another measure of spread and is equal to the square root of the variance;

5   be familiar with the following results:

<table>
<tr><td align="center">**For raw data**</td><td align="center">**For frequency distributions**</td></tr>
<tr><td align="center">$$\bar{x} = \frac{\sum x}{n}$$</td><td align="center">$$\bar{x} = \frac{\sum fx}{\sum f}$$</td></tr>
<tr><td align="center">$$\text{variance} = \frac{\sum (x - \bar{x})^2}{n}$$</td><td align="center">$$\text{variance} = \frac{\sum f(x - \bar{x})^2}{\sum f}$$</td></tr>
<tr><td align="center">$$\text{or } \frac{\sum x^2}{n} - \bar{x}^2$$</td><td align="center">$$\text{or } \frac{\sum fx^2}{\sum f} - \bar{x}^2$$</td></tr>
</table>

6   know that:

  (a) if each value is multiplied by a constant a, then the standard deviation is also multiplied by a,

  (b) if each value is increased by adding on a constant b, then the standard deviation is unchanged.

Standard deviation and variance

The ice dance scores

for couple A	5.7	5.8	5.7	5.8	5.8	5.8

for couple B	4.8	5.2	4.9	5.8	5.5	5.8

1 For couple A, find the total squared distance from the mean value (to 2 s.f.).

2 Calculate the variances for couple A and couple B.

3 Obtain the standard deviation of the scores for each couple.

4 Obtain by direct calculation the standard deviation for each data set below and comment on how well the standard deviation seems to measure spread.

(a)   5, 5, 5, 5, 5, 5, 5   (b)   1, 2, 3, 4, 5

(c)   1, 2, 3, 4, 5, 6   (d)   2, 4, 6, 8, 10

5 Investigate, by considering a number of data sets, what happens to the mean and the standard deviation when

(a) all the values in the data set are increased by the same value, for example 2, 5, 7 becomes 12, 15, 17;

(b) all the values are multiplied by the same number, for example 2, 5, 7 becomes 6, 15, 21.

Write down your conclusions.

Variance by direct calculation

Having an algebraic form for the variance means that you can, by some manipulation, consider other ways of expressing the result.

The variance formula is

$$\text{Variance} = \frac{\sum (x - \bar{x})^2}{n}$$

An algorithm for direct calculation of the variance using this result is illustrated.

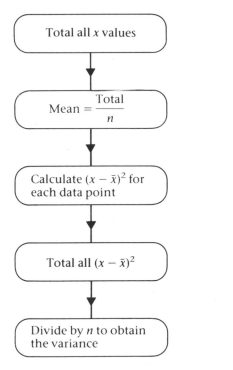
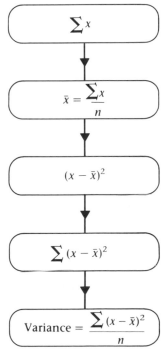

1 Use this algorithm to calculate the variance of the following values.

(a) 2.1, 3.8, 3.9, 6.2

(b) 30, 29, 47

Comment on any difficulties in obtaining the variance using this algorithm.

The algorithm provided is not efficient and you might look for an alternative expression.

Consider only two data values a and b.

$$\bar{x} \;=\; \frac{1}{2}\,(a + b)$$

$$\text{Variance} \;=\; \frac{1}{2}\left[(a - \bar{x})^2 + (b - \bar{x})^2 \right]$$

Expand, as a quadratic in $\bar{x}$,

$$\text{Variance} = \frac{1}{2}\left[a^2 - 2a\bar{x} + \bar{x}^2 + b^2 - 2b\bar{x} + \bar{x}^2 \right]$$

$$\Rightarrow \text{Variance} = \frac{1}{2}\left[a^2 + b^2 - 2\bar{x}\,(a + b) + 2\bar{x}^2 \right]$$

But $a + b = 2\bar{x}$ so,

$$\text{Variance} = \frac{1}{2}\left[a^2 + b^2 - 4\bar{x}^2 + 2\bar{x}^2 \right]$$

$$\text{Variance} = \frac{a^2 + b^2}{2} - \bar{x}^2$$

2   Obtain a result in this form for three data values a, b, c.

3   Conjecture a result for

   (a) four data values a, b, c, d

   (b) n data values

4   Use your result to re-calculate the variance of the two data sets in question 1. Comment on the way in which this algorithm is easier to use than the earlier one.

5   Write an algorithm in the form of a flow chart for your result in question 3. If you are interested in computer programming you might like to write a program which uses your algorithm to work out the variance of n data values.

4 Probability models 1

4.1 Introduction

'When a piece of toast drops to the floor, it usually lands buttered-side down' (Murphy's law!).

Statistical data need careful interpretation. As in this illustration, they tell a story, but opinions can differ about what the story means.

> (a) Does the evidence in the cartoon prove Murphy's law?
>
> (b) Would Murphy's law be proved if 70 out of 100 pieces landed butter-side down?
>
> (c) Use the random number generating function on a computer or programmable calculator to simulate the situation described in the illustration. Help is given on technology datasheet: *Toast*.

In order to assess the significance of data objectively, you need to construct **probability models** for the circumstances which generate the data. In this chapter you will learn how to construct probability models for some simple cases.

4.2 Order from chaos

In the beginning . . .
how the heavens and
earth rose out of chaos.

Milton

The outcome of events in real life is often unpredictable. When a coin is tossed, heads and tails occur at random. No one can yet predict whether the act of conception will produce a male or a female. Although the motion of individual gas molecules is random, the distribution of large numbers of molecules can be described and predicted by physical laws.

In all these cases, although the outcome of individual events is random, the accumulation of large numbers of similar events produces patterns. Over many trials, a coin (unlike toast!) will tend to fall as many times on one side as on the other side, and about half the numbers of babies born are girls.

TASKSHEET 1 — Chance cards 1 (page 69)

Statistical data can often be regarded as outcomes of repeating the same process, measurement or experiment a number of times. For each outcome, you can calculate

the **frequency** : how often it occurs,
the **relative frequency** : the frequency divided by the number of trials.

Although outcomes occur randomly, the relative frequency appears to become close to a fixed number, between 0 and 1, as the number of trials increases. This number, the **probability**, gives a measure of the likelihood of a particular outcome at each trial:

likelihood impossible certain

probability 0 1

Sometimes you can calculate a value for the probability by arguing that there is a set of outcomes which are 'equally likely'. Often in statistics it is not possible to do this, and you can only propose values for probabilities based on relative frequencies or past experience.

The outcome of statistical enquiries or experiments often produces numerical data. For example, when a die is thrown, the outcome produced is a number from 1 to 6; a traffic survey produces a number of vehicles per minute; weather data produces the number of inches of rainfall per day; a survey of family size might be used to investigate the number of children per family, or annual income. In all these cases, the outcome is a variable which has a set of possible values.

The value which the variable takes for any particular throw of a die, or vehicle count, or day's rainfall, etc., is essentially random: you cannot predict with certainty what its value will be. These variables are therefore called **random variables**.

Random variable	Set of possible values
Score on a die	1, 2, 3, 4, 5, 6
Number of vehicles per minute	0, 1, 2, . . .
Rainfall in inches	Any positive real number
etc.	. . .

It is usual to denote a random variable by a capital letter, for example X, and the particular values it can take by lower case letters, for example $x_1, x_2, x_3, \ldots, x_n$. So if a random variable, S, is the score on a die, the particular values it can take are $s = 1, 2, 3, 4, 5, 6$.

On tasksheet 1, you selected a card at random from a chance card pack. The number you obtained varied randomly from 1 to 4. You can therefore say that each of the letters Y, R, B, G, used to stand for the outcome of selecting from the yellow, red, blue or green pack, is an example of a random variable, taking the values 1, 2, 3 or 4.

For each pack, you worked out the probability of getting each value of the random variable. For example, for the yellow pack:

y	1	2	3	4
$P(Y = y)$	0.4	0.3	0.2	0.1

This is called the **probability distribution** for the random variable Y. In general, the probability distribution for a random variable is a statement (or table) which assigns probabilities to the possible values of the variable.

Sometimes, probabilities are assigned by arguing that the possible outcomes are equally likely. But in other cases, you may need to estimate the probabilities from relative frequencies, or from past experience.

For any probability distribution, the sum of the probabilities must equal 1.

Explain why the sum of the probabilities must equal 1.

E X A M P L E   1

A family with two children is chosen at random. The random variable X stands for the number of boys. Assume each child is equally likely to be a boy or girl.

(a) Write down the probability distribution for the random variable.

(b) Draw a graph of the probability distribution.

S O L U T I O N

(a) Considering the sex of the children (youngest followed by eldest) gives a set of four equally likely outcomes {(B,B) (B,G) (G,B) (G,G)}

Only one of the four possible outcomes gives two boys,

so $P(x = 2) = \frac{1}{4}$

Two possible outcomes result in just one boy in the family,

so $P(x = 1) = \frac{2}{4}$

By a similar argument

$P(x = 0) = \frac{1}{4}$

x	0	1	2
$P(X = x)$	0.25	0.5	0.25

Notice that the three possible values for X are **not** equally likely and that the sum of the probabilities equals 1. The most likely number of boys is 1.

(b) As X can only take discrete values, the most appropriate form of graph is a **stick graph**.

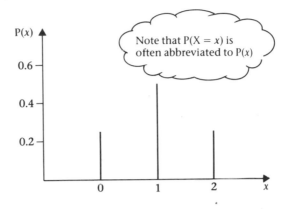

Note that $P(X = x)$ is often abbreviated to $P(x)$

EXERCISE 1

For each of the following random variables, either calculate its probability distribution or estimate it using relative frequencies calculated from the data given. Check also that the sum of the probabilities in each distribution is 1.

1 S = score obtained throwing an unbiased die.

2 X = number of children in a family chosen from the following population:

Number of children x	0	1	2	3	4 or over
Number of families f	123	179	457	88	45

3 S = score when a coin is tossed, counting 0 for a head and 1 for a tail.

4 Y = value of a playing card cut from a pack, counting 1 for an ace, and 10 for a ten, Jack, Queen or King.

5 T = duration of a telephone call:

Duration (min) t	0–1	1–2	2–3	3 or over
Number of calls f	230	420	480	358

4.3 Random variables: discrete or continuous?

As you have seen, there are two fundamentally different types of distribution of quantitative data: continuous and discrete. Similarly, there are the same two types of probability model.

In exercise 1 the question on telephone calls concerned a **continuous** random variable. The duration of a call can theoretically take any real number value (within reasonable limits for telephone calls). On the other hand, all the other variables are **discrete**. They cannot be said to vary continuously. For example, the number of children in a family must be a whole number.

From a certain population, one family (which includes at least one child) is sampled. Consider the following random variables:

- C = number of children in the family;

- H = height of eldest child;

- S = size of shoe worn by mother;

- T = number of natural teeth for the father;

- W = weight of youngest child;

- G = proportion of children who are girls;

- A = age of youngest child.

Which of the variables above are:

(a) continuous;   (b) discrete?

The rest of this unit will concentrate on random variables which are discrete, since their probability distributions are easier to characterise mathematically. Models for continuous random variables are considered in some of the other statistics units. However, you should be aware of the distinction between these two types of random variable.

4.4 The mean and variance of a random variable

In chapters 2 and 3, you used the **mean** as a representative value for a set of data. For a sample of values of a variable X you calculated this using the formula

$$\bar{x} = \frac{\sum xf}{n}$$

Σ stands for 'the sum of'.

where f is the frequency of the value x, and n is the total number of values. As the frequency f divided by the total number of values n is the relative frequency, you can rewrite this formula using relative frequencies:

$$\bar{x} = \sum x \left(\frac{f}{n}\right)$$

So to calculate the mean, you multiply the values of x by their relative frequencies, and sum over all values of x.

EXAMPLE 2

Using relative frequencies, calculate the mean of the following data set: 1, 1, 2, 3, 3, 3, 3, 3, 4, 4.

SOLUTION

x	1	2	3	4	
f	2	1	5	2	$n = 10$
$\dfrac{f}{n}$	0.2	0.1	0.5	0.2	

$$\text{Mean} = \sum x \left(\frac{f}{n}\right)$$
$$= 1 \times 0.2 + 2 \times 0.1 + 3 \times 0.5 + 4 \times 0.2$$
$$= 2.7$$

The next tasksheet uses this formula to calculate means for the data you collected from the 'chance card' simulation on tasksheet 1.

TASKSHEET 2 – Chance cards 2 (page 70)

For any discrete random variable X, the mean is defined as

$$\mu = \sum x\, P(x)$$

This means that to find the mean of a discrete random variable, you multiply the values of X by their probability, and add. Compare the formulas for sample distributions and probability distributions:

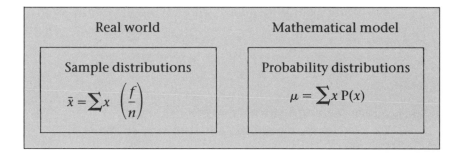

For probability distributions, the relative frequencies are replaced by the probabilities. For large samples, relative frequency and probability are likely to be close, and get closer as the sample size gets larger and larger. From the formulas above, the same is true for $\bar{x}$ and μ, that is

> As the sample size increases, the sample mean $\bar{x}$ is likely to be close to the mean μ of the random variable.

The ideas used to calculate the mean of a random variable from its probability distribution can also be applied to the variance.

The variance of a frequency distribution can be redefined in terms of relative frequency.

$$\text{variance} = \frac{\sum x^2 f}{n} - \bar{x}^2$$

$$= \sum x^2\left(\frac{f}{n}\right) - \bar{x}^2$$

Replacing relative frequency with probability gives a formula for the variance of the random variable. The symbol σ^2 is used to denote this variance to distinguish it from the sample variance which is given the symbol s^2.

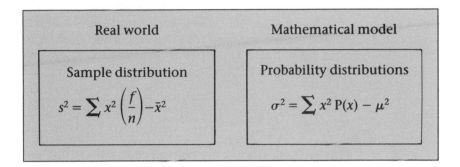

Real world	Mathematical model
Sample distribution	Probability distributions
$s^2 = \sum x^2 \left(\dfrac{f}{n}\right) - \bar{x}^2$	$\sigma^2 = \sum x^2 \, P(x) - \mu^2$

E X A M P L E   3

Calculate (a) the mean and (b) the variance of the number of boys in a family of two children.

S O L U T I O N

(a) The mean

n	0	1	2
P(n)	0.25	0.5	0.25

$$\mu = \sum n \, P(n)$$
$$= 0 \times 0.25 + 1 \times 0.5 + 2 \times 0.25$$
$$= 1$$

Using this probability model, you can predict that for a large sample of families with two children, the mean number of boys per family will be approximately 1.

(b) The variance
$$\sum n^2 \, P(n) = 0^2 \times 0.25 + 1^2 \times 0.5 + 2^2 \times 0.25$$
$$= 1.5$$
$$\sigma^2 = \sum n^2 \, P(n) - \mu^2 = 1.5 - 1^2$$
$$= 0.5$$

According to this probability model, you can predict that for a large sample of families with two children, the variance of the number of boys will be approximately 0.5.

Working through calculations for mean and variance a few times should give you a 'feel' for the meaning of these important statistical formulas. However, to save time spent on laborious 'number-crunching', you may already have been tempted to see if the statistical function keys of your calculator will work out means and variances for random variables, just as they did for data. The answer is that they can! All that is required is for probabilities to be entered instead of frequencies.

EXERCISE 2

For questions 1, 2, 3 in this execise you should calculate the mean and variance **without** using the statistical functions on your calculator.

1   The random variable *D* has the value obtained from a single roll of an unbiased die. Write down the probability distribution for *D*, and calculate the mean and the variance.

2   There are five coins in a bag, one 50p coin, two 20p coins and two 10p coins. One coin is withdrawn at random. Calculate the mean value of the amount withdrawn and the variance.

3   Calculate the mean and variance of the score for each of the spinners shown below.

(a) 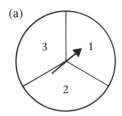 (b) 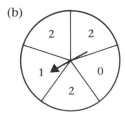 (c)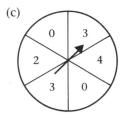

4   A card is withdrawn at random from a pack of playing cards. Counting 1 for an ace and 10 for a Jack, Queen or King, calculate the mean and variance of the value of the card withdrawn.

5   Naresh walks to work two days in five, cycles two days in five, and takes the bus one day in five. The walk takes 45 minutes, cycling takes 20 minutes and the bus 15 minutes. Define a random variable to model this situation, and hence calculate the mean journey time.

6   Is it better to invest £100 in premium bonds, or in fixed interest savings (such as a building society or national savings investment account)? To answer this, you will need some information about the number and values of premium bond prizes, and the chances of winning one.

In February 1987, there were 1856 million £1 bonds in the draw and 168 701 prizes, with the following values, awarded every month.

Prize value (£)	50	100	500	1000	5000	10000	25000	50000	100000	250000
Frequency	155073	10373	2412	800	25	5	4	4	4	1

The probability of a single bond winning a £50 prize one month is

$$\frac{155073}{1856 \times 10^6} = 8.355 \times 10^{-5}$$

(a) Copy and complete the table of probabilities.

Prize value (£) w	0	50	100	500	1000	5000	10000	25000	50000	100000	250000
$P(w)$		8.355×10^{-5}									

(b) Calculate from this table the mean of W, the random variable which represents the amount won by a premium bond.

(c) How much, on average, would the expected winnings per £1 bond be in one year? How does this compare with a fixed interest investment paying, say, 10% per annum?

7 (a)

In a game of 'shove ha'penny', a player projects a penny to land on the grid shown. Assume that the penny lands at random inside the frame, and the amount scored is the amount in pence shown in the square containing the centre of the coin. Work out the expected gain.

(b) Suppose all the coins must land inside a square before winning, and that the side of each square is twice the diameter of the coin. By considering the area of the square within which the centre must lie for the coin to land entirely in the square, work out the probability that this happens. Deduce what the expected gain is now.

4.5 Simulations

You have already used the microcomputer to simulate random events, such as dropping toast and cutting packs of cards. Simulations are widely used to generate data for situations which are too complicated to analyse mathematically, or for which a 'real' experiment would be too costly or dangerous.

Behind each simulation lies a **probability model.** Two examples are offered, one from physics and one from biology. Neither assumes any technical knowledge. Select one of these to try. You may like to try to construct a microcomputer simulation of your own.

TASKSHEET 3 OR 4 — *The nuclear reactor (page 71)*
The fly (page 73)

After working through this chapter, you should:

1. appreciate that probabilities lie between 0 and 1 and can be calculated by considering equally likely outcomes or estimated using relative frequencies;

2. understand the terms random variable and **probability distribution** and be able to construct simple probability models;

3. appreciate the difference between **discrete** and **continuous random variables**;

4. be able to calculate the **mean** and **variance** of a discrete random variable and understand their significance;

5. be able to use a computer to perform a simple **probability simulation.**

Chance cards 1

You will need: Chance cards
                 Recording Sheet 1: Chance cards
                 A computer and the statistics software

Each of the coloured packs contain 40 cards numbered 1, 2, 3 or 4, in different proportions. Do not inspect the packs!

1 (a) Select the yellow pack, cut it randomly 50 times, and record the number of 1s, 2s, etc. in the table provided on recording sheet 1.

   (b) Calculate the relative frequency of 1s, 2s, etc. by dividing the frequency by the total number of cuts. Enter these in the table and complete the stick graph.

   (c) What can you say about the composition of the yellow pack?

2 The sampling of the packs is simulated by the program 'Chance cards'.

   (a) Use the program to cut the yellow pack 100, 500 and 1000 times. Enter the results on the recording sheet, and complete the graph.

   (b) Estimate the probability of cutting each number. Can you guess what the composition of the pack is? How sure are you of your guess?

   (c) Now confirm your hypothesis by inspecting the pack. Calculate the probabilities from the composition of the pack.

3 For each of the other two packs (red and blue), investigate the probability distribution of the value of a card selected at random. Try a few cuts to get a 'feel' for the composition (but don't bother to cut the pack 50 times). Then use the program to fill in the table for 100, 500 and 1000 cuts, and confirm the distribution by inspecting the pack. Finally, write down the probabilities on the recording sheet.

4 A fourth pack of 40 cards, the green pack, is simulated by the program. Find out what you can about the composition of this pack.

Chance cards 2

You will need your results from tasksheet 1.

Suppose you are to be 'banker' in the following game. You ask the player to select a card at random from the yellow pack. You pay out £y, where y is the number on the card selected. The mean winnings per game is given by the formula

$$\bar{y} = \sum y \left(\frac{f}{n} \right)$$

1   Use your figures from tasksheet 1 to work out the mean winnings for the 100, 500 and 1000 games played with the yellow pack.

What would be a reasonable amount to charge for each game?

2   Out of 1000 games, you would expect, 'on average', 400 £1 payouts, 300 £2 payouts, 200 £3 payouts and 100 £4 payouts.

y	1	2	3	4	
f	400	300	200	100	$n = 1000$
$\dfrac{f}{n}$	0.4	0.3	0.2	0.1	

Achieving this precise result is, of course, unlikely, but it is the distribution you might 'expect' from the probability distribution. Work out the mean of these winnings.

The 'expected relative frequencies' are simply the probabilities. So this mean value is simply the sum of the values of Y multiplied by their probabilities:

$$\text{mean} = \sum y \, P(Y = y)$$

This mean represents the average winnings from a game. It is called the **mean of the random variable Y**, and is often denoted by the greek letter μ ('mu'). To break even in the long run, you should charge this amount per game.

Notice that the mean of the random variable is **fixed**, whereas the sample mean $\bar{y}$ varies according to the sample values.

3   (a)   Calculate, from the probability distribution, the mean μ of the random variable R, where R represents the value of a cut from the red pack.

    (b)   Now calculate the sample means $\bar{r}$ for the results of 100, 500 and 1000 cuts of the red pack you collected on tasksheet 1. Compare these with the value of μ.

4   Repeat question 3 for the random variable B, where B represents the value obtained from a cut of the blue pack. Again, use the data you collected on tasksheet 1.

The nuclear reactor

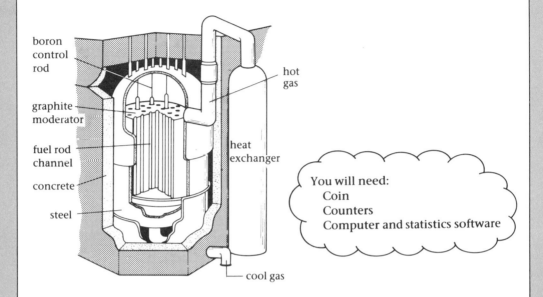

boron control rod

graphite moderator

fuel rod channel

concrete

steel

hot gas

heat exchanger

cool gas

You will need:
Coin
Counters
Computer and statistics software

When a free neutron hits and is captured by a uranium 235 nucleus, the nucleus nearly always splits up and releases one or more neutrons.

Assuming for simplicity that each fission produces two neutrons, then the first fission produces two free neutrons and successive 'generations' of free neutrons would consist of 4, 8, 16 neutrons, and so on. In a nuclear bomb the number of free neutrons rises rapidly and there is a catastrophic release of energy. In a nuclear reactor, free neutrons can be absorbed in nuclei which do not split up and power is produced in a controlled way.

The rate at which the reaction proceeds depends upon the chances of an individual neutron being absorbed, or colliding to produce more free neutrons. A simple model can be constructed as follows.

1   Apparatus: counters, coin.

Start with 10 counters. These will represent the initial number of free neutrons. The fate of each neutron is decided by the toss of a coin: a head means it collides, producing two free neutrons; a tail means it is absorbed. So in this model, it is **assumed** there is an equal probability of collision and absorption.

Pick up the first counter, and toss the coin. If you get a tail, discard it; if you get a head, pick up a spare counter, and place the two aside for the next round. Repeat for each of the 10 counters.

In round 2 repeat the process for the 'neutrons' generated in round 1. Continue for 5 rounds, or until there are no counters left.

Record your results in a copy of the table below. t_n, t_a and t_c are running totals for neutrons tested, absorbed and collided, and n the neutrons left.

Round	Neutrons tested so far (t_n)	Absorptions so far (t_a)	Collisions so far (t_c)	Neutrons left (n)
1				
2				
3				
4				
5				

Do you think that the reaction simulated would increase, die out or continue at a constant rate? Discuss for different numbers of initial free neutrons.

2 Load the program 'Nuclear 1'. In this program, you input the initial number of free neutrons, the probability of collision and the number of rounds. The table produced is as in 1, but in addition the ratio $t_c : t_n$ is calculated after each round. This represents the total number of collisions divided by the total number of neutrons trialled.

(a) Run the program initially with 100 neutrons and probability of collision

(i) 0.4   (ii) 0.6   (iii) 0.5

Write down what you notice.

(b) Repeat with probability of collision 0.5 and initially

(i) 10 neutrons   (ii) 50 neutrons   (iii) 500 neutrons

Comment.

3 Suppose a neutron collides with probability p and is absorbed with probability $1 - p$. Let X be the number of free neutrons generated by a random free neutron.

(a) Write down the probability distribution of X and show that the mean value is $2p$.

(b) Use this to explain the results of your simulations in 2(a).

4 Suppose now that a neutron collides with probability p, and that collision can produce either one or two free neutrons, with equal probabilities. Find the value of p which would give a stable reaction. This situation is simulated by the program 'Nuclear 2'. Load this, and check your results.

5 Comment on the limitations of this model.

The fly

You will need: Die
Counters
Computer and statistics software

A population of flies can be modelled as follows. Each fly lives exactly one week, at the end of which each female reproduces. Between 0 and 3 of the offspring are female.

Suppose the probability distribution for the number of females produced by each female fly is as follows:

y	0	1	2	3
$P(Y = y)$	$\frac{1}{3}$	$\frac{1}{3}$	$\frac{1}{6}$	$\frac{1}{6}$

1 Take 10 counters. These will represent the initial population of females. Determine the number of female offspring by throwing a die, as follows:

Score on die	1 or 2	3 or 4	5	6
y	0	1	2	3

Run through the initial population, adding or rejecting counters as appropriate. Simulate 5 generations. Is the population increasing or decreasing? Will the population survive?

2 The population model is simulated by the program 'Fly'. Enter the probability distribution given above and investigate what happens with initially

(a) 1 female

(b) 10 females

(c) 100 females

73

3 Calculate the mean of the random variable Y with the probability distribution above. How does this confirm the results of your simulations?

4 For each of the following distributions, work out the mean number of females produced, and predict whether the population explodes, declines or is stable:

	P(0)	P(1)	P(2)	P(3)
(i)	0.5	0.1	0.4	0
(ii)	0.2	0.6	0.1	0.1
(iii)	0.1	0.8	0.1	0
(iv)	0.5	0	0.5	0

Which of populations (iii) and (iv) is most vulnerable? (Hint – consider the variance.)

5 Confirm your predictions using the program 'Fly'.

6 Comment on any limitations of the probability model.

5 Probability models 2

5.1 Multiplying probabilities

In using probability models it is often necessary to consider outcomes of events which are combinations of simpler events.

For example, for a darts player to score 180 with three darts requires the combination of the events of scoring 60 with each dart.

Suppose that the darts player above hits treble 20 with one dart in five on average.

What is the probability of her scoring 180 with three darts?

Comment on any assumptions you have made.

If two events are such that *the occurrence of one does not affect the probability of the other occurring*, they are called **independent events**.

The probability of two independent events both occurring can be found by multiplying their individual probabilities.

EXAMPLE 1

Three coins are tossed. What is the probability of obtaining three tails?

SOLUTION

The tosses are independent events and so:

$$P(T\,T\,T) = P(T) \times P(T) \times P(T)$$
$$= 0.5 \times 0.5 \times 0.5$$
$$= 0.125$$

5.2 Adding probabilities

Many events depend upon one or other of two simpler events occurring. This is illustrated on tasksheet 1.

TASKSHEET 1 — Snap (page 91)

The following example is solved by counting cases and demonstrates a general rule for adding probabilities in such cases.

EXAMPLE 2

A card is selected from an ordinary pack. What is the probability that the card is either an ace or a diamond?

SOLUTION

There are 52 possible cards that could be chosen; 4 of these are aces, 13 are diamonds.

There are only 16 cards which are either aces or diamonds because the ace of diamonds is counted in both the 4 aces and the 13 diamonds.

$$\text{P(ace } or \text{ diamond)} = \frac{4 + 13 - 1}{52} = \frac{4}{13}$$

The solution to example 2 can be written as

$$\text{P(ace } or \text{ diamond)} = \frac{4}{52} + \frac{13}{52} - \frac{1}{52}$$

$$= \text{P(ace)} + \text{P(diamond)} - \text{P(both ace } and \text{ diamond)}$$

This is a particular example of the **addition law**:

For any two events A and B, the probability of either A or B occurring is

$$\text{P}(A \text{ } or \text{ } B) = \text{P}(A) + \text{P}(B) - \text{P}(A \text{ } and \text{ } B)$$

The addition law is especially simple when events A and B are **mutually exclusive**, i.e. both cannot occur, because then $\text{P}(A \text{ and } B) = 0$.

Discuss whether the following pairs of events are mutually exclusive and whether they are independent.

(a) The weather is fine; I walk to work.

(b) I cut an ace; you cut a king.

(c) Dan's Delight wins next Saturday's 2:30 race at Newbury; Andy's Nag wins next Saturday's 2:30 race at Newbury.

(d) Dan's Delight wins next Saturday's 2:30 race at Newbury; Andy's Nag wins next Saturday's 3:15 race at Newbury.

(e) Mrs Smith has toothache today; Mr Smith has toothache today.

(f) Mrs Smith has a cold today; Mr Smith has a cold today.

You can use the addition law to work out the probability of an event **not** occurring from the probability of it occurring. For example, suppose that the probability of a bus being late is 0.1. Then the probability of it being on time is 0.9. This is because the events 'bus late' and 'bus on time' are mutually exclusive, and because one or other of the events **must** occur.

Use the addition law to justify this last statement.

In general, given an event A and its opposite A',

$$P(A') = 1 - P(A)$$

where $P(A')$ is the probability that A does **not** occur.

This is often a useful problem-solving tool for working out probabilities; if you cannot work out the probability of an event directly, see if you can work out the probability of the opposite event, then subtract this from 1.

EXAMPLE 3

Three coins are tossed. What is the probability of at least one head?

SOLUTION

There are lots of ways of getting at least one head. But the only way of getting the opposite event, namely no head at all, is to toss three tails.

$$P(T\,T\,T) = 0.5 \times 0.5 \times 0.5 = 0.125$$
$$P\text{ (at least 1 head)} = 1 - P(T\,T\,T) = 0.875$$

EXAMPLE 4

I travel by bus and train on my journey to work. The probability that the bus is late is 0.3 and (independently) the probability that the train is late is 0.2. Calculate the probability that

(a) the bus and train are late

(b) either the bus or the train is late.

SOLUTION

(a) P(bus and train late) = P(bus late) × P(train late)
$$= 0.3 \times 0.2 = 0.06$$

(b) P(bus or train late) = P(bus late) + P(train late) − P(both bus and train late)
$$= 0.3 + 0.2 - 0.3 \times 0.2 = 0.44$$

EXERCISE 1

1 In a board game two dice are rolled. Work out the probability of

(a) a double six   (b) at least one six   (c) only one six.

2 A card is selected from a pack of ordinary playing cards. What is the probability that it is

(a) a red ace   (b) a six or a seven

(c) either an ace or a Queen?

3 A card is selected from an ordinary pack of 52 cards. What is the probability that it is

(a) a heart or a six   (b) a heart or a spade?

4 A coin is tossed and a pack of playing cards cut. What is the probability of getting

(a) a head or a Jack   (b) a head and a Jack?

5.3 Tree diagrams

When analysing the probabilities of a combination of events, a tree diagram often helps.

EXAMPLE 5

A show jumping course contains a triple combination of jumps consisting of a wall, a gate and parallel bars. Previous statistics suggest that the probabilities of successfully negotiating each jump are 0.8, 0.7 and 0.9 respectively. Each fence knocked down incurs a penalty of four faults. Ignoring the chance of refusals, calculate the probability of getting four faults in total when jumping this combination.

SOLUTION

You can represent the situation with a tree diagram as follows:

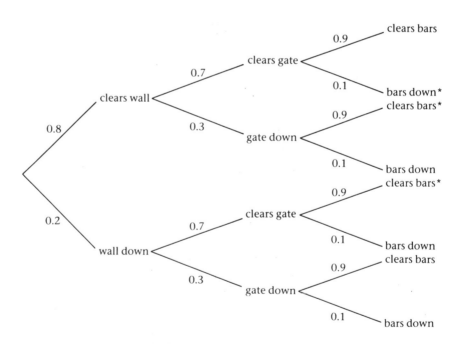

To find the probability of a particular sequence of events, **multiply** the probabilities on the branches.

Why can you multiply the probabilities in this case?

For example, P (clears wall, fails gate, clears bars) = $0.8 \times 0.3 \times 0.9$
$$= 0.216.$$

To obtain the probability of a total of four faults, you should **add** the probabilities on the branches representing 'one fence down'. These are marked with a star on the tree diagram. The answer required is therefore

$$0.8 \times 0.7 \times 0.1 + 0.8 \times 0.3 \times 0.9 + 0.2 \times 0.7 \times 0.9$$
$$= 0.398.$$

Why can you add these probabilities?

EXERCISE 2

1   For the example above, work out the probability distribution of the random variable F = number of faults.

2   It is perhaps more realistic to assume that the horse has a higher chance of failing at a fence if it has put the previous fence down. Suppose you model this assumption by adjusting the probabilities as follows: if the previous jump is down, increase the probability of failing with the next jump by 0.1.

Draw a tree diagram, and calculate the probability of

(a) no faults   (b) 4 faults.

3   Trish selects a card at random from a pack of playing cards, and replaces it. She repeats this three times.

(a) Calculate the probability of her getting

(i)   three hearts   (ii)   three cards of the same suit.

(b) Suppose she selects the three cards without replacement. Re-calculate the probabilities for (a).

4   Assuming that giving birth to a boy or a girl is equally likely, construct a tree diagram to show the possible outcomes of the sexes of children in a family with three children. Hence find the probability of

(a) exactly one girl

(b) at least one girl

(c) at least one child of each sex.

5.4 The binostat

This is a binostat. It is like a
pinball machine. Balls are fed in
at the top, fall through a
triangular grid and collect in a
series of slots. The picture shows
the distribution in the slots after a
number of balls have passed
through the grid. If you have a
binostat available, drop 50 balls
through the grid and observe the
distribution you get.

 The picture shows that more balls collect in the central slots than
in the outside slots. Why do you think this happens?

 TASKSHEET 2 — The binostat (page 92)

The results of tasksheet 2 can be summarised as follows:

(a) The number of routes to each position or slot is given by the
following triangle, where each number is the sum of the
numbers in the previous row immediately to the left and to the
right:

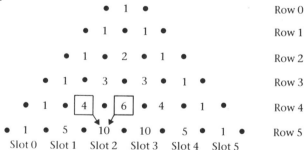

			• 1 •				Row 0
		• 1 • 1 •				Row 1
	• 1 • 2 • 1 •				Row 2
• 1 • 3 • 3 • 1 •				Row 3
• 1 • 4 • 6 • 4 • 1 •				Row 4
• 1 • 5 • 10 • 10 • 5 • 1 •				Row 5

Slot 0   Slot 1   Slot 2   Slot 3   Slot 4   Slot 5

(b) For a binostat with n rows (not counting the first row of pins),
there are 2^n equally likely paths and the probability of a ball
following one particular path is $1/2^n$.

You can use the results of (a) and (b) to find the probability
distribution for a ball's final position.

You may already recognise this triangle of numbers from previous
work. It is known as Pascal's triangle, after the French
mathematician Blaise Pascal (1623–1663), whose deeply held
religious beliefs did not hold him back from a study of the calculus
of chance inspired by his interest in gambling!

The sort of probability distribution you found for the binostat occurs quite often. Before finding the circumstances in which it arises, you will need a generalised interpretation of the numbers in the triangle.

Consider this three-row binostat:

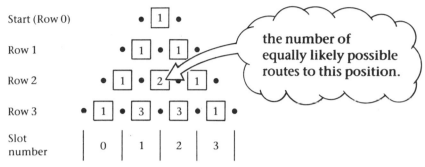

Start (Row 0)

Row 1

Row 2

Row 3

Slot number

the number of equally likely possible routes to this position.

Notice that the 'slot number' just gives the number of times the ball is deflected to the right in its path to the slot. So, for example, to get to slot 2, the ball must be deflected twice to the right (and hence once to the left) out of the total of three deflections. So the number of routes to slot 2 is simply the number of ways of choosing two deflections out of three to be 'right' i.e. L R R, R L R and R R L.

Similarly, the entry '10' in slot 2 of row 5 gives the number of ways of choosing 2 'right' deflections out of 5. It could equally give the number of ways of getting 2 heads from 5 tosses, or choosing 2 presents from 5 presents, or more generally choosing 2 things from 5. This number is written as $\binom{5}{2}$. You can now use Pascal's triangle to work out similar probability distributions.

E X A M P L E   6

A coin is tossed. Find the number of ways, and hence the probability, of getting

(a) exactly two heads from three tosses;

(b) exactly two tails from six tosses.

S O L U T I O N

(a) There are $\binom{3}{2} = 3$ ways of choosing two heads from three tosses,

namely H H T, H T H and T H H. As there is a total of eight (2^3) possible outcomes, the probability is

$$P\,(2\text{ heads}) = 3 \times \frac{1}{8} = \frac{3}{8}$$

83

(b) Six tosses have $2^6 = 64$ possible equally likely outcomes.

Two tails can occur $\binom{6}{2}$ ways, which is obtained as row 6, slot 2 of the triangle.

$$\begin{array}{ccccccccc} & & & & \text{Slot 2} & & & & \\ \text{Row 6} & 1 & 6 & \textcircled{15} & 20 & 15 & 6 & 1 \end{array}$$

$$\Rightarrow \binom{6}{2} = 15$$

$$\Rightarrow P\,(2\text{ tails}) = 15 \times \frac{1}{64} = \frac{15}{64}$$

EXERCISE 3

1 Extend the triangle as necessary to work out

(a) the number of ways of choosing 4 objects from 7 like objects;

(b) $\binom{7}{4}$ (c) $\binom{6}{4}$ (d) $\binom{5}{2}$

(e) $\binom{2}{1}$ (f) $\binom{7}{3}$ (g) $\binom{5}{4}$ (h) $\binom{5}{5}$

2 A coin is tossed 7 times. In how many ways can you get exactly

(a) 3 heads   (b) 4 tails?

Explain your answers. What does this tell you about Pascal's triangle?

3 A pack of playing cards (without jokers) is cut eight times. What is the probability of cutting a red card on six occasions?

4 Assuming that boy and girl births are equally likely, what is the probability that a family of four children will contain three or more girls?

5 In a nuclear reaction, a free neutron has an equal chance of being absorbed or colliding to produce a fission. What is the probability that out of five free neutrons

(a) all will be absorbed;

(b) all but two are absorbed?

6 A bag contains equal numbers of white and red marbles. Ten players draw a marble from the bag and replace it. What is the probability that precisely five players draw a white marble?

5.5 Unequal probabilities

So far, you have modelled the probabilities for repetitions (or trials) of an event with two possible outcomes (for example head or tail, boy or girl, etc . . .) which are assumed to be equally likely to occur. You have found that the probability of r outcomes from n trials is

number of choices of r from n × probability of each choice

$$= \binom{n}{r} \times \frac{1}{2^n}$$

What if the two outcomes are not equally likely?

This is equivalent to a binostat which is not properly balanced, so the probability of deflecting to the left is greater than to the right. The distribution of balls in the slots becomes 'skewed', i.e. there are more balls in the left hand slots than the right.

TASKSHEET 3 — The biased binostat (page 94)

You can now generalise the probability model to all situations when

- there are n repetitions or trials of an event, the outcomes of which are **independent**;

- the probability of a particular outcome is fixed;

- you are counting the number of times this outcome occurs.

The probability distribution for the random variable R is found by

(a) working out the probability of a sequence containing r occurrences out of n,

(b) then multiplying by the number of ways of getting this outcome, namely $\binom{n}{r}$.

Probability models of this type occur frequently enough to merit a name of their own. They are called **binomial probability** models.

85

EXAMPLE 7

Three fair dice are thrown. What is the probability of throwing two sixes?

SOLUTION

The probability of, say, (six) (no six) (six) is

$$\frac{1}{6} \times \frac{5}{6} \times \frac{1}{6}$$

So the probability of two sixes is $\binom{3}{2} \times \frac{1}{6} \times \frac{5}{6} \times \frac{1}{6} = \frac{5}{72}$

EXAMPLE 8

On average 90% of seeds from a particular packet germinate. If you plant ten seeds in a row, what is the probability of eight or more germinating?

SOLUTION

The probability of, say, the first eight germinating and the last two dying is

$$0.9 \times 0.9 \times \ldots \times 0.9 \times 0.1 \times 0.1 = (0.9)^8 (0.1)^2$$

Extending Pascal's triangle to row 10 shows that the number of ways of getting exactly eight germinations is

$$\binom{10}{8} = 45$$

So the probability of eight germinations is

$$45 \times (0.9)^8(0.1)^2 = 0.1937 \text{ (to 4 s.f.)}$$

Similarly, the probability of nine germinations is

$$10 \times (0.9)^9 \times 0.1 = 0.3874$$

and of all the ten germinating is

$$1 \times (0.9)^{10} = 0.3486$$

So the total probability of eight or more is

$$0.1937 + 0.3874 + 0.3486 = 0.93 \text{ (to 2 s.f.)}$$

What assumptions are being made in this binomial model?

How valid do you think these are?

EXERCISE 4

1 Four dice are thrown. Calculate the probability distribution for S, the number of sixes thrown.

2 Bob is not much good at darts. On average, he misses the board one time in three. Bob has three darts to throw. Model the situation with a binomial distribution, using a random variable D for the number of darts which land on the board.

3 'Eight out of ten prefer Wizzo to Wow' is the sort of claim advertisements sometimes make. It could be based on one sample of ten people only!

(a) Assume that Wizzo is no better or worse than Wow. Work out the probability that out of a random sample of ten people who were offered the choice, eight or more prefer Wizzo to Wow.

(b) Assume Wizzo is in fact preferred by 80% of people. Work out the probability that out of a random sample of ten people, eight or more prefer Wizzo to Wow.

4 Birth statistics show that 52% of babies born in Britain are male. Use this to calculate the probability that a family of four children will contain three or more girls.

5 Boat Race statistics to date show that Oxford have won on 54% of occasions. Use a binomial model to calculate the probability that Cambridge win three times in a period of five years. Do you think the model is appropriate in this case? Explain.

5.6 Making inferences

The binomial probability distribution can be summarised as follows:

> Given n trials of an event, the probability of r occurrences of an outcome which has a probability p of occurring at each trial is
>
> $$\binom{n}{r} p^r (1 - p)^{n-r}$$
>
> assuming that the trials are independent.

You can now model the toast-dropping experiment at the start of chapter 4.

On the assumption that the outcomes of 'butter up' and 'butter down' are equally likely, the probability of seven slices out of ten landing 'butter down' is

$$\binom{10}{7} (0.5)^7 (0.5)^3 = 0.117$$

The full probability distribution for the random variable R, the 'number of "butter down" slices out of ten' is given below:

r	0	1	2	3	4	5	6	7	8	9	10
$P(R = r)$	0.001	0.010	0.044	0.117	0.205	0.246	0.205	0.117	0.044	0.010	0.001

$$P(R = r) = \binom{10}{r} 0.5^r 0.5^{10-r}$$

Notice that no result in itself has a high probability.

> In making a test of this kind, explain why it is sensible to consider a result of **seven or more** slices landing 'butter down'.

From the table the probability of seven or more slices landing butter-side down is $0.117 + 0.044 + 0.010 + 0.001 = 0.172$

So, on the assumption that Murphy's law is incorrect, you can expect a result of seven or more 'butter down' slices out of ten on about one in six occasions. This is quite often, and so the result is not very significant evidence in favour of Murphy's law.

Calculating the likelihood of getting 70 or more out of 100 'butter down', given an equal chance of landing either way, is explored in a later statistics unit. The probability of this result is about 0.001, and observing such an event **would** be strong evidence in support of Murphy's law.

EXERCISE 5

1 (a) Five poker dice have six faces marked ace, King, Queen, Jack, 10 and 9. What is the probability of throwing three or more aces?

   (b) A player gets three or more aces three times out of four throws. Calculate the probability of this event.

2 A cricket captain wins the toss nine times out of ten. Investigate how lucky this is.

3 Weather statistics for Blackpool in July suggest that it rains one day in three. The Wilsons take a week's holiday there in July, and it rains on six days out of seven. Use a binomial model to estimate how unlucky this is. Is the model appropriate?

4 In a test of a new recipe for a soft drink, eight people sampled a glass of new and a glass of old. Out of these, seven preferred the new flavour, and one the old. How strong is this evidence that the new recipe is in fact better?

5 A rare plant is difficult to grow. Each seed has a 20% chance of germinating.

   (a) If I plant five seeds, what chance is there that at least one will germinate?

   (b) Investigate how many seeds I should plant to get a 90% chance of at least one germination.

After working through this chapter you should:

1 understand the term **mutually exclusive** as applied to events, and appreciate when it is appropriate to add probabilities;

2 understand when two events are statistically **independent** and when it is appropriate to multiply probabilities;

3 be able to use **tree diagrams** to analyse the probability of compound events;

4 know how to apply the **binomial distribution** to model appropriate situations;

5 know that, if the random variable R gives the number of occurrences of an event with probability p out of n independent trials, then

$$P(R = r) = \binom{n}{r} p^r q^{n-r} \text{ where } q = 1 - p;$$

6 understand how probability models can be used to make **inferences**.

Snap

Two children are playing 'snap' with the Chance cards. One has a yellow pack (16 ones, 12 twos, 8 threes and 4 fours) and one has a red pack (10 each of ones, twos, threes and fours). The packs are well shuffled and each child plays her top card simultaneously.

1 There are 40 cards in each pack. What is the total number of pairs of cards which could be played?

2 (a) How many of these are 'double ones'; that is a one from the yellow pack and a one from the red pack?

   (b) How many are

   (i) double twos;   (ii) double threes;   (iii) double fours?

   (c) How many are doubles (i.e. double anything)?

For equally likely outcomes, the probability of an event is

$$\frac{\text{the number of outcomes which correspond to the event}}{\text{the total number of possible outcomes}}$$

So the probability of a double one is

$$\frac{\text{the number of possible 'double ones'}}{\text{the total number of pairs}}$$

3 Use this principle and your answers from question 2 to work out the probability of

   (a) a double one;   (b) a double two;   (c) a double.

The probability distributions for the two packs are as follows:

Yellow pack

Number	1	2	3	4
Probability	0.4	0.3	0.2	0.1

Red pack

Number	1	2	3	4
Probability	0.25	0.25	0.25	0.25

4 How could you work out the probabilities in question 3 directly from the probability distributions?

5 The blue pack has 10 ones, 20 twos, 10 threes and no fours. Working directly from the probability distributions, calculate the probability of a 'snap' if a yellow pack is played against a blue pack.

The binostat

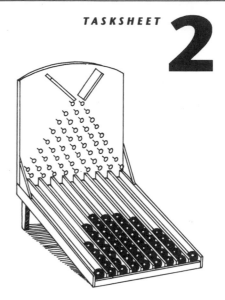

The program 'Bino' simulates a binostat. You can enter the number of rows of pins (not counting a first row of two pins), the probability of a ball deflecting to the right at each pin and the number of balls to be 'dropped'. The slots are numbered from the left, starting with 0 for the left-hand slot, 1 for the next right, and so on.

Select 3 rows and probability of moving right 0.5 (so there is an equal chance of a ball deflecting left or right).

Run the program using 10, 100 and 400 balls, to get a 'feel' for the distribution of the balls which build up in the slots.

You should find that roughly three times as many balls fall into the central slots (numbered 1 and 2) as the outside slots (0 and 3). To investigate this, consider a ball which falls into slot 2. One possible route which the ball could take is shown.

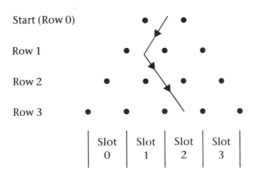

1   Find how many different routes the ball could take to slot 2. What is the probability of each route? Deduce the probability of a ball falling into slot 2.

2   Repeat this calculation for slots 0, 1 and 3, and hence write down the probability distribution of the random variable X, where X = slot number.

3   Use this to predict the expected frequencies in each slot when 400 balls are used, then simulate this with the program 'Bino' (taking 400 balls). Compare the results with the expected frequencies.

4   This is a binostat with two rows. By considering the number of routes to slots 0, 1 and 2, find the probability distribution of X = slot number.

Run a simulation with 400 balls, and compare the observed and expected frequencies.

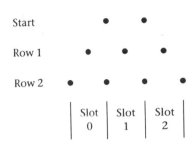

For a larger number of rows, you need a way of calculating the number of routes to each slot. Consider this binostat with four rows.

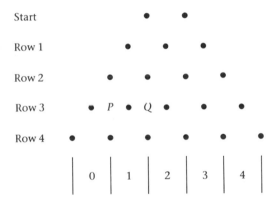

5   Find the probability of taking any particular route through this binostat.

To find how many routes there are to, for example, slot 1, you can use the fact that all routes to this slot pass through either P or Q (see diagram).

6   By writing down the number of routes to points P and Q, deduce how many routes there are to slot 1 and hence the probability of a ball falling into this slot.

7   Repeat the argument for the other slots and hence write down the probability distribution for X = slot number in this case.

8   Run a simulation with 4 rows and 400 balls and compare the simulated frequencies with the expected frequencies from the probability distribution.

The biased binostat

You will need a computer and the program 'Bino'.

A binostat with three rows is tilted so that for each deflection there is a probability of 0.6 of the ball going left (and hence 0.4 of going right).

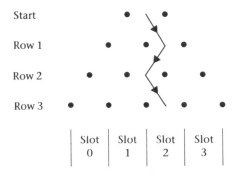

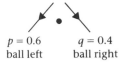

$p = 0.6$ $q = 0.4$
ball left   ball right

1 Calculate the probability of a ball taking the route shown above to slot 2. What assumption are you making when you multiply the probabilities for each deflection?

2 Calculate the probability of a ball falling into slot 2 by any other route.

3 Calculate the probability of a ball falling into slot 2.

4 Repeat the calculation for slots 0, 1 and 3 and hence find the probability distribution of X = slot number.

5 Calculate the expected frequencies if 500 balls are sent down this binostat. Conduct a simulation with 500 balls and compare the simulated frequencies with the expected frequencies.

6 Calculate the probability distribution for 5 rows, with $p = 0.6$ as before.

7 Calculate the probability distribution for X with $p = 0.2$ and 3 rows.

6 Sampling

6.1 Introduction

The illustrations demonstrate three particular examples of
sampling. They are:

- taking a 'taster' from a vat of wine;

- road testing a vehicle, perhaps to assess its safety characteristics in a
  collision;

- surveying opinions by direct questioning – market research perhaps.

A central problem of statistics is how to use information from a
sample to infer whatever one can about the **parent population**
from which the sample is taken.

By considering the illustrations above and some examples of
your own, think of various different reasons why you might want
to use a sample rather than test every member of the population.

What makes for a 'good' sample?

6.2 **Bias in sampling**

The following two problems involve particular sampling procedures which are **not** good!

P R O B L E M   1

At a particular railway station the trains run hourly in each direction. However, when a traveller arrives at a random time at this station, the next train is five times more likely to be eastbound than westbound.

> Can you explain this curious result?

P R O B L E M   2

A mythical king decided to choose between his daughter's various suitors and boost the palace renovation fund by asking each of his prospective sons-in-law to contribute as many gold coins as they could to the fund.

The coins were marked with the suitors' names and were placed by the princess in a couple of urns. The king then chose at random an urn and a coin from that urn.

The princess' favourite suitor was very poor and could only contribute one coin to the thousands that were collected.

> How could the princess legitmately improve her favourite's chances and what precisely would his chances then be?

Sampling procedures such as those in problems 1 and 2 are **biased**. The 'next train' was not likely to be repesentative of all the trains and the apparently random method of selecting a coin proved to be similarly flawed.

When attempting to draw conclusions on the basis of a particular sample it is vital to consider whether the method of selecting the sample is likely to have introduced bias.

It is sometimes helpful to think of a sample as providing a 'window' through which you can see a small part of the unknown population – called the **parent** population.

To enable reliable information to be obtained about a population from a sample, it is important to be careful about **how** the sample is chosen.

TASKSHEET 1 — Bias (page 104)

One important requirement of a sample is that every member of the population has an equal chance of being selected. The sample members are **selected at random.**

EXERCISE 1

In each of the following examples, decide what bias, if any, the sampling procedure has introduced.

1 George Anderson is an accountant for a large company and works on the third floor of a twelve-storey building. He frequently has to visit the computer room on the tenth floor and travels up and down using one of the lifts. He often grumbles about the lifts and says, 'When I'm on the third floor waiting to go up, the first lift that comes is usually going down, whereas when I want to come back down again the first lift to arrive is usually going up'.

2 To obtain information about diseases amongst the elderly, everyone in a large residential home was given a thorough health check.

3 In the US Presidential Election of 1948, a major telephone opinion poll predicted a victory for the Republican, Dewey, over the Democrat, Truman.

4 A headmistress was asked to prepare a report for the school governors on the reasons for absences from school: illness, interviews, truancy, etc. Part of the report was based upon a full investigation of all absences during a week in November.

6.3 Sample size

Ensuring that the sample members are selected at random is not the only requirement of a good sample.

> What useful information can be obtained from a sample of one?

Clearly, the more information you can obtain, the better your inferences will be.

 TASKSHEET 2 — Sample size (page 105)

Larger samples are **more likely** to give more reliable information about a population. This conclusion has an element of common sense about it. A sample of 10 is **likely** to be better than a sample of 5.

> Why would you expect a sample of 20 to be better still?

A more interesting question is how large the sample needs to be to give reliable information about the population. Public opinion polls, for example, always state sample size as well as the method used to select the sample. The sample size is generally about 1200 people.

When studying reports of sampling procedures you must consider both whether the sample has been chosen in a random way and whether the sample is sufficiently large for any results to be significant.

Canvassing 'everyone' is so costly and time-consuming that sampling is a widespread technique, despite the inevitable problems.

> The sample should be selected at random. Any hint of possible bias should be avoided.
>
> The sample must be large enough to provide sufficiently accurate information about the population.

The concepts relating to sampling techniques and the inference of results from samples will be developed and made more precise in the optional statistics units of this course.

6.4 Testing claims by simulation

Reports on surveys are very common in advertising and in the local and national press. You have seen that you must always consider both how the sample is selected and whether or not the sample is large enough for the results to have any real significance.

The article below is reprinted from the *Southampton Guardian* of Wednesday 13 May 1987.

You throw out monorail idea

By Mark Hodson

COUNCIL plans for a £20m futuristic monorail through the centre of Southampton have been given a thumbs down from city residents.

According to a Guardian readers' survey, 90 per cent of people do not want the new 'Metro 2000' system, and almost half would prefer to see the return of trams to the city.

Of those responding, 10 per cent said they want the monorail, 48 per cent want the trams back and 42 per cent said neither idea was worth taking up.

The Metro 2000 would join 13 central stations with electrically-driven remote controlled modules carrying up to 20 people at a time.

The proposals are not yet council policy, but are being used as the basis for discussions with local groups.

A report summarising views of local people will be compiled later this year, and the council is now keen to gauge public response before then.

Tory leader Cllr Norman Best, who has branded the monorail "a gimmick", said the council should think again in the light of the results of our poll.

"These figures do not surprise me at all," he said. "When all these people have taken the trouble to write in, they should be listened to. I am convinced the majority of people in Southampton do not want this monorail, but would prefer to see the return of the trams."

Council leader Alan Whitehead wrote in his introduction to the plans: "I am aware that such an innovation may fundamentally change the face of the city. An understanding and agreement across the city of exactly where we are going and what steps we need to take to get there will immensely strengthen the hand of whoever is charged with taking such decisions."

He says the scheme has met with an enthusiastic response from developers who he hopes will put up the £20m needed.

There will be a public meeting on June 1 when council officers will answer questions about the details of the plans.

WHAT YOU SAY:

● "A definite NO to the city-wrecking, crazy idea of a monorail, which would benefit no-one," said J Gubb, Bedford Place.

● "I am against the monorail, trams and any other gimmicks by aspiring Westminster residents. Surely the priority must be to improve existing services," said S Hunter, Radstock Road.

● "Trams would add to noise pollution. A monorail would be much more exciting and would attract visitors to the city," said M Buckle of Rushington Lane.

● "A monorail is a ridiculous idea. It would completely ruin the appearance of the city. The supporting structures would certainly look awful, and the noise for those people working in adjoining buildings would be unbearable," said Mrs J Draper of Chilworth.

● "Bring back the trams. They are cheap to ride, cheap to run and efficient as transport can be," said Alfred Hole of Peach Road.

● Our poll attracted 48 replies.

(a) Which people would you expect to be in favour of a monorail in the centre of a city?

(b) How many replied and of those who replied, how many wanted

(i) the monorail   (ii) the trams   (iii) neither?

The article uses the views from a sample of the residents to judge the general support, or lack of support, for the monorail idea. Such sampling is widely used for purposes as varied as market research on proposed new products, establishing views about changes in public services, quality control in manufacturing processes and judging public opinion before elections.

In any sampling procedure it is important that the way the poll is carried out should not introduce bias. For example a poll conducted by telephone would exclude approximately one fifth of the population. This could be a crucial omission.

(a) What do you understand the word 'bias' to mean?

(b) How do you think the monorail 'poll' was carried out? Would this method introduce bias in the sample? Suggest a better method.

A second important consideration for any sampling procedure is connected with the sample size. How reasonable is it to infer from a sample size of only 48 that the majority of the inhabitants of Southampton are opposed to the monorail? Is it possible that the citizens are divided roughly equally on this issue and that the sample result occurred simply by chance?

The probability that such a result could have occurred simply by chance can be calculated using the binomial distribution. If you assume that 50% of the population are in favour of the monorail, the probability that a random sample of 48 shows only 5 or fewer in favour would be

$$\binom{48}{5}\left(\frac{1}{2}\right)^{5}\left(\frac{1}{2}\right)^{43} + \binom{48}{4}\left(\frac{1}{2}\right)^{4}\left(\frac{1}{2}\right)^{44} + \ldots + \binom{48}{0}\left(\frac{1}{2}\right)^{0}\left(\frac{1}{2}\right)^{48}$$

This would not be easy to calculate!

TASKSHEET 3 — Simulations (page 106)

A computer can be used to simulate a poll several times and you can then see from the simulation how likely particular occurrences appear to be.

A simulation of the monorail poll in which the poll is carried out 100 times is shown below.

Distribution of simulated samples

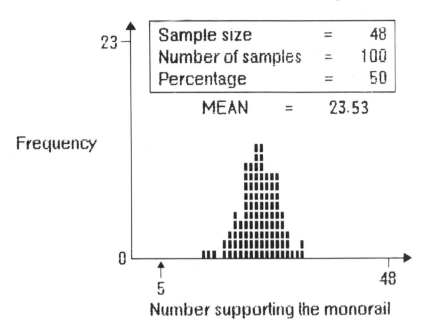

This shows that in a poll of 48 people, obtaining 5 or fewer in support of the project is very unlikely. The poll would therefore provide strong evidence that the majority of the population are against the monorail **if** you could be confident that the method of conducting the poll has not introduced bias into the sample.

6.5 Further testing

Using the ideas of this chapter, you can investigate some of the claims typically made in television and newspaper advertising. For example, a television commercial states that 8 out of 10 dogs prefer Wolfit dogfood. The claim is based upon a particular test in which 8 out of 10 dogs chose Wolfit when given a choice between Wolfit and another dogfood.

What would the manufacturer of Wolfit like you to infer from this claim?

Does the survey of dogs support the intended inference?

A complaint is made by rival dog food manufacturers that the commercial is misleading. They say that 8 out of 10 dogs choosing Wolfit would not be an unusual occurrence if it is assumed that dogs have no particular preference for Wolfit. The assumption that dogs have no preference for either dog food implies that they will choose either one or the other at random. The probability of choosing Wolfit is 0.5 on the basis of this assumption. The probability of 8 or more dogs out of 10 choosing Wolfit can be obtained from the binomial distribution.

> Why is a binomial model suitable in this situation?

The probability that exactly 8 choose Wolfit is

$$\binom{10}{8}\left(\frac{1}{2}\right)^8\left(\frac{1}{2}\right)^2 = \frac{45}{1024}$$

If R is the number choosing Wolfit, then the full probability distribution is

r	0	1	2	3	4	5	6	7	8	9	10
$P(R = r)$	$\frac{1}{1024}$	$\frac{10}{1024}$	$\frac{45}{1024}$	$\frac{120}{1024}$	$\frac{210}{1024}$	$\frac{252}{1024}$	$\frac{210}{1024}$	$\frac{120}{1024}$	$\frac{45}{1024}$	$\frac{10}{1024}$	$\frac{1}{1024}$

> What is the probability that 8 or more dogs in a sample of 10 will choose Wolfit?

The result '8 or more out of 10' is only likely to occur in about 5% of all samples of 10 dogs. This is not very likely and suggests that the assumption made by the rival manufacturers is probably wrong. It appears likely that more than 50% of dogs would indeed choose Wolfit.

EXERCISE 2

1 A person claims that he can predict which way a coin will land, either heads or tails. In eight throws he gets it right on six occasions.

Calculate, on the basis of a binomial model, the probability of

(a) getting six correct out of eight;

(b) getting six or more correct out of eight.

Do you think the result supports his claim? Explain your answer.

2 A blind tasting is organised to see if people can tell the difference between two different brands of orange juice. They have ten 'tastes'. On each occasion they have to say whether it is juice A or juice B.

On how many occasions would you expect them to get it right before you were reasonably convinced that they could actually tell the difference?

After working through this chapter you should:

1 appreciate the need for sampling and for ensuring that the sampling procedure does not introduce bias;

2 know how to check significance either by simulation or, when appropriate, by using the binomial distribution;

3 be aware that as the sample size increases the distribution of the sample mean becomes increasingly clustered around the true value of the population mean.

Bias

> You will need: Datasheet 2: Heights
> Sampling windows
> Recording sheet 2: Bias

Although the heights listed on datasheet 2 form a fairly small group, this will be used as an example of a population from which samples can be selected. The aim of the experiment is to see what happens if, in order to estimate the mean height of this population of 300 sixth formers, you take a sample and find the sample mean height.

SAMPLING EXPERIMENT 1

Take a sample of five heights by placing window A anywhere on the datasheet. Record the five sample values on recording sheet 2 and calculate the mean height for this sample.

Now repeat the procedure using window B. You now have two different estimates of the population mean height.

Collect the results from the whole group so that you obtain a distribution of sample means using sampling window A and another for sampling window B. (At least fifty results are necessary and you may need to obtain several samples for windows A and B to ensure sufficient data.)

The population mean height for the entire group of 300 sixth formers is actually 167.4 cm.

1 How close were your sample estimates?

2 How close were the estimates gained by the rest of the class?

3 Which 'window' gave the better results?

4 What criticisms do you have of the sampling procedure used in this experiment?

5 How could it be improved?

Sample size

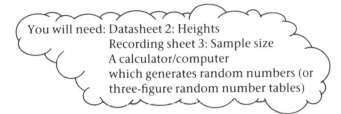

You will need: Datasheet 2: Heights
Recording sheet 3: Sample size
A calculator/computer
which generates random numbers (or
three-figure random number tables)

SAMPLING EXPERIMENT 2

Use three-figure random numbers to select from the datasheet a random sample of five students' heights. If using a random number table, each student should use a different part of the table.

1 Why should each student use a different part of the table?

Record your results on recording sheet 3 and calculate the mean height of your sample. Repeat this for two more samples of size five and then for three samples of size ten.

Finally collect up the results for the entire group by recording all the sample means on the tables provided. (At least fifty results are necessary in each case.)

2 Do the samples give similar distributions to those obtained using the windows on tasksheet 1? What are the main differences?

3 Draw histograms of the distributions you obtain for the sample means of:

(a) random samples of size five;

(b) random samples of size ten.

Calculate the mean and variance of all the sample means for (a) and (b).

4 How close are these to the population mean of 167.4 cm?

5 Calculate the variances of the two distributions of sample means (for random samples).

(a) Which size of sample produced better estimates of the population mean?

(b) Which distribution of sample means was least variable?

(c) Comment on how the difference in spread of the two sample means affects your ability to infer results from a particular sample mean.

Simulations

You will need: The statistics program *Sampling*.

The *Sampling* program enables you to test conjectures based upon the results from a particular sample.

- First make an assumption about the parent population to enable you to simulate the taking of samples. You might, for example, assume that 50% of the population support a particular measure such as the construction of a monorail.

- Then simulate the selection of a large number of samples of the same size as the actual sample.

- From the distribution of the simulated samples you can use the actual sample to judge the reasonableness of the original assumption.

The result of a simulation, where 100 samples of size 48 were taken, is shown below:

Distribution of simulated samples

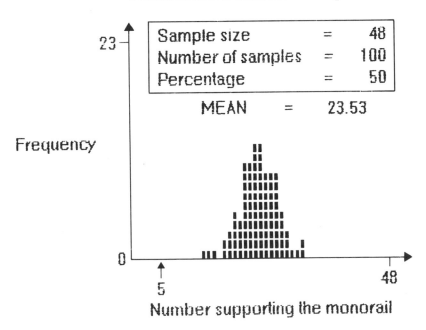

1   Do you think the initial assumption of 50% supporting the monorail is likely, considering the simulation result?

2 (a) Run the program yourself and check that you obtain a distribution similar to the one printed on the previous page.

   (b) Explain why you would expect your distribution to be slightly different from the printed example.

3 Suppose that a randomly selected *Southampton Guardian* sample had contained 22 people in favour of the monorail. What conclusion would you reach in this case?

Use the program when answering the following questions.

4 A particular brand has 40% of the cola market. After a television advertising campaign, a survey of fifty teenagers shows that twenty-five of them now drink this brand. Decide whether or not the campaign has been successful and give your reasons.

5 (a) If a coin comes down heads three times out of ten throws, would you suspect it was biased? Explain your answer.

   (b) A coin is tossed one hundred times and comes down heads thirty times. Would you suspect this coin to be biased?

Comment on your conclusions to (a) and (b).

6 A particular die is rolled ninety times and only eight sixes are obtained. Is it biased?

Solutions

1 Statistics and probability

1.2 Order from chaos

> Illustrate the four cases.

①	②③ ④	②	①③ ④	③	①② ④	④	①② ③

> With four molecules, how many different cases are there altogether?

There are 16 cases.

4 : 0 split	1
3 : 1 split	4
2 : 2 split	6
1 : 3 split	4
0 : 4 split	1
	16

A neat way of seeing that there are 16 cases is to note that each molecule has two possible positions, left or right. The number of cases is therefore

$$2 \times 2 \times 2 \times 2 = 16$$

2 Exploratory data analysis

2.2 Stem and leaf display

> From this back-to-back stem plot, what would you deduce about the relative temperatures of Bournemouth and Torquay?

Bournemouth seems a little warmer and possibly has less variation in the temperature.

> What impression of the data can be obtained from stem and leaf plots?

Stem and leaf plots provide a visual impression of the data from which it is possible to get an idea of the middle or average value, the extreme values and the spread.

EXERCISE 1

1   Sunshine hours in Bournemouth and Torquay (July 1987)

Bournemouth		Torquay	
4	15	1	
1 0	14	5	
6 3 1	13	5 7	
	12	3	
8 0	11	5 5	
6 1	10	0	
	9		
7 7 0	8	8	
	7	6 8 8	
9	6	9	
	5	1 1 5	
4	4	6	
9 2	3	0 8	
8 7 6	2	0 2 3	
6	1	6	
5 2 2	0	5 7	

13|5 means 13.5 hours of sunshine

You can conclude that there is not much difference between the towns.

2 Examination marks

	Class 1		Class 2	

```
                            9 │ 1
                7   4   0    8 │ 0  1  3
    9  8  8  6  6  5   1      7 │ 1  3  3  5  9
       9  6  5  4  2   0      6 │ 2  4  4  8  9
          9  8  6  3   1   0  5 │ 1  5  6  8  9
                             4 │ 5  8
                          1  3 │ 4
```

6|4 means 64 marks

(a) Disregarding the 91 mark in class 2, class 1 seem to have done marginally better, with more marks in the upper 70s and 80s.

(b) Both have approximately symmetrical distributions. The marks for class 1 are slightly more closely bunched than those for class 2.

3 Graduate starting salaries

```
16 │ 0
15 │ 0
14 │ 0
13 │ 0  0
12 │ 0  0  0
11 │ 0  0  0  0
10 │ 0  0  0  0
 9 │ 0  0  0  5
 8 │ 0  0  5  5
 7 │ 0  5
```

10|0 means £10000

The distribution is skewed towards the lower end. The bulk of salaries are in the range £7000–£13000, but there are a few very highly paid jobs. The median is £10000.

2.3 Numerical representation of data

> Give reasons why each of the following numbers could be said to *represent* the data set above:
>
> 5.2, 5.3, 5.29.

5.2 is the most frequently occurring score.

5.3 is the middle value when the scores are ranked in increasing order of size.

5.29 is the mean, the sum of all the scores divided by 9.

EXERCISE 2

1 Mean $= \frac{1}{50}(41 \times 0 + 6 \times 1 + 3 \times 2) = \frac{12}{50}$

Mode $= 0$ Median $= 0$

The mode is most sensible measure of the average in this case.

2 (a) Mean $= \frac{1052}{19} = 55.4$ seconds (to 3 s.f.)

Median $= 52$ seconds

It would probably be better to quote the mean as this better reflects the individual values, some of which are very low and some high.

(b) Although the person did not complete the jigsaw it should be included. It will significantly affect the mean – if you credit this person with a time of 148 seconds the new mean is 60 seconds. The median is much less affected by an extreme value such as this. (Here, in fact, it is still 52 seconds.)

3 The distribution has two peaks – it is bimodal. Any of the measures of average might be used, but data such as these emphasise that you need to know more about a population than simply a measure of its average value, which can disguise a great deal of hidden detail. There is no particular merit in any of the measures here.

2.4 Box and whisker diagrams

> Describe some of the features of the box plot above.

The whiskers are of unequal length.

The median is towards one end of the box.

EXERCISE 3

1   The range of A is greater overall although it has a smaller interquartile range. The average speed of B is greater than that of A. B has a relatively symmetric distribution whereas A's is skewed.

2   (a) The highest recorded temperature was 83 °F, in Copenhagen. London was generally hotter, with a median temperature of 66 °F against Copenhagen's 63 °F. London's lower quartile is only 1 °F less than Copenhagen's upper quartile.

    (b) Copenhagen had the greater range of temperatures overall even though the interquartile range for London is much greater than that for Copenhagen. The interquartile range is not particularly useful when planning a trip – you need the full range when deciding what to pack. From that point of view, Copenhagen is the more variable.

    London has a more symmetric distribution than Copenhagen.

3   (a) E is the most reliable. 50% of the scripts required at most a $\frac{1}{2}$ mark adjustment.

    (b) Drop examiner C, who has greater variability than others in the box section. It is not very easy to make a general adjustment.

    (c) Decrease every mark by one.

2.5   Constructing box plots

> Obtain from the graph the median and the quartiles for the length of stay for male patients.

Median   = 8 days
Upper quartile = 11 days
Lower quartile = 5 days

> Find the upper quartile using this technique.

The upper quartile is between the 38th and 39th patient from the top – both were in hospital for 11 days, so the upper quartile is 11 days.

> Obtain the equivalent box plot for females. Draw the two box plots on the same scale and use them to compare the lengths of stay for male and female patients. Comment also on the shapes of the two distributions based on the evidence of the box plots.

For females, the following is obtained:

Median = 8 days
Upper quartile = 14 days
Lower quartile = 3 days

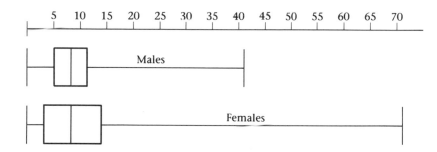

Typical male and female patients stay the same length of time – 8 days. However, the length of stay for female patients is more variable. 50% of female patients stay between 3 and 14 days whereas 50% of males stay between 5 and 11 days. Both distributions are asymmetric, having long tails to the right.

> Find the median for females and the remaining quartiles for both sets of reaction times given above.

Reaction times in seconds

	Males	Females
Upper quartile	0.22	0.230
Median	0.185	0.210
Lower quartile	0.165	0.170

EXERCISE 4

1 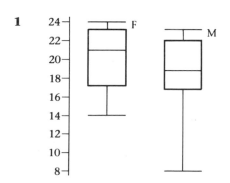 The average reaction time is lower for males. The distribution of times for males is more variable.

2 The 'box' for class 1 is slightly higher, showing that they have done better overall.
The 'box' for class 2 is smaller, showing that they are a more evenly matched group, even though their range is slightly larger.

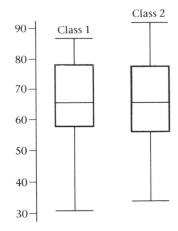

3

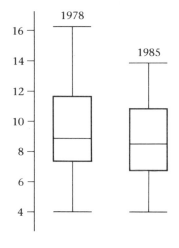

Total alcohol consumption has dropped slightly.

4 (a) There was very little sunshine in January. There was a much more varied amount in July.

(b)

	January	July
(i) Median	0.4	5.7
(ii) Lower quartile	0	2.6
(iii) Upper quartile	2.1	7.7

(c)

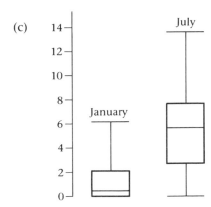

(d) There was a much greater range of sunshine hours in July and the average sunshine was much higher. In January there was no recorded sunshine on at least a quarter of the days.

3 Data analysis revisited

3.1 Introduction

> Draw a stem and leaf diagram for the data about the metropolitan districts. Comment on the suitability of a stem and leaf diagram for this data.

Number of households lacking at least one basic amenity (per 1000 households) for metropolitan districts

```
29 |  3
28 |  9
27 |  0
26 |
25 |
24 |  7  8
23 |  8
22 |  3
21 |  0
20 |  0  0  1  1  6  6
19 |  1  5
18 |  2  3  3  6  8
17 |  5
16 |  4
15 |  4  6  8  8
14 |  6
13 |  4  8
12 |  3
11 |  3  6  8
10 |
 9 |
 8 |
 7 |
 6 |
 5 |
 4 |  4
 3 |
 2 |  5
```

9|1 means 191 substandard households (per 1000 households)

The stem and leaf diagram still gives a useful pictorial representation. It is, however, tedious to construct, even with the relative small data set in datasheet 1.

3.2 Grouping data

> What should you consider when deciding what group widths to use?
>
> Group the data on the metropolitan districts from datasheet 1 into a grouping of your choice.

If the intervals are too narrow, then it can be difficult to notice any features of the data. The extreme case of an interval of width 1 should illustrate this point! Conversely, if the intervals are too wide then much of the information contained in the data will be lost.

There is no one 'correct' grouping of the data on the non-metropolitan counties. You should apply the principles above when choosing your grouping.

3.3 Representing grouped data – histograms

> Does the diagram provide a good representation of the data?
>
> Justify your answer.

No. It gives the impression of a large number of screws in the 0–20 mm range. Worse, it suggests that there are 5 screws of length 0–5 mm, another 5 of length 5–10 mm and so on. In fact there are only 5 in the whole 0–20 mm range!

> Which type of diagram best illustrates the distribution? Explain why.

The frequency density diagram is best because there is no distortion as there was in the earlier diagram. This sort of diagram must be used when data is grouped into unequal class intervals.

3.4 Problems with data

> Under what circumstances would this decision be reasonable?

It seems likely that some of the 8 observations in the 30+ group are greater than 39, otherwise the data would all fall in the interval 30–39 and this would have been given as the group size.

Taking a width of 20 might be reasonable for many streets although it would not be appropriate if, for example, the survey took place near a factory gate at the end of a shift.

EXERCISE 1

1 (a) (i) $10 \times 1 = 10$ (ii) $10 \times 2 = 20$ (iii) $20 \times 1 = 20$

(b) Total frequency = 50

2 Total frequency = $(25 \times 0.2) + (50 \times 0.4) + (50 \times 0.2) = 35$

3 (a)

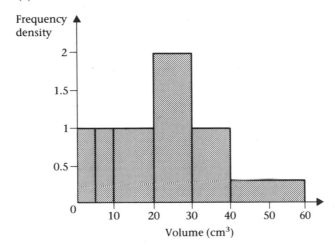

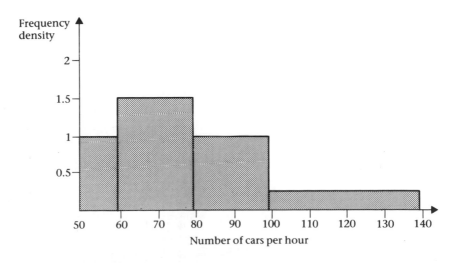

4 (a) See the table in (b). The choice of grouping should reflect the principles established in the previous discussion.

(b)

Rainfall (mm)	Width	North		South	
		Frequency	Frequency density	Frequency	Frequency density
40–69	30	1	$\frac{1}{30} = 0.033$	10	$\frac{10}{30} = 0.33$
70–79	10	4	$\frac{4}{10} = 0.4$	9	$\frac{9}{10} = 0.9$
80–89	10	9	$\frac{9}{10} = 0.9$	11	$\frac{11}{10} = 1.1$
90–99	10	4	$\frac{4}{10} = 0.4$	8	$\frac{8}{10} = 0.8$
100–109	10	11	$\frac{11}{10} = 1.1$	6	$\frac{6}{10} = 0.6$
110–119	10	6	$\frac{6}{10} = 0.6$	4	$\frac{4}{10} = 0.4$
120–129	10	5	$\frac{5}{10} = 0.5$	1	$\frac{1}{10} = 0.1$
130–139	10	1	$\frac{1}{10} = 0.1$	0	0
140–149	10	5	$\frac{5}{10} = 0.5$	0	0
150–229	80	4	$\frac{4}{80} = 0.05$	1	$\frac{1}{80} = 0.012$

As the readings are to the nearest mm, the true intervals are 39.5–69.5, 69.5–79.5, etc. The positioning of the bars on the histogram should reflect this.

(c)

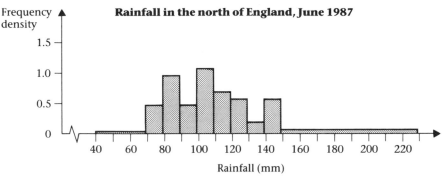

Rainfall in the north of England, June 1987

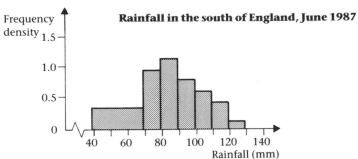

Rainfall in the south of England, June 1987

(d) The south of England has more readings in the 40–69 mm range and in general appears to have had a drier month than the north of England. This result needs to be interpreted cautiously as it does not mean that the south has a drier climate than the north. It only indicates what happened in one particular month.

The 100 weather stations chosen were fairly equally divided between the east and the west of England to avoid any east–west differences affecting the result. The line from the Wash to the Bristol Channel was chosen as the north–south boundary for the purposes of this study.

5   One possible grouping would be:

Number of households (per 1000)	Width	Non-metropolitan counties		Metropolitan districts	
		Frequency	Frequency density (2 s.f.)	Frequency	Frequency density (2 s.f.)
20–59	40	0	0	2	$\frac{2}{40} = 0.05$
60–99	40	4	$\frac{4}{40} = 0.10$	0	0
100–119	20	5	$\frac{5}{20} = 0.25$	3	$\frac{3}{20} = 0.15$
120–139	20	7	$\frac{7}{20} = 0.35$	3	$\frac{3}{20} = 0.15$
140–159	20	9	$\frac{9}{20} = 0.45$	5	$\frac{5}{20} = 0.25$
160–179	20	7	$\frac{7}{20} = 0.35$	2	$\frac{2}{20} = 0.10$
180–239	60	7	$\frac{7}{60} = 0.12$	16	$\frac{16}{60} = 0.27$
240–299	60	0	0	5	$\frac{5}{60} = 0.08$

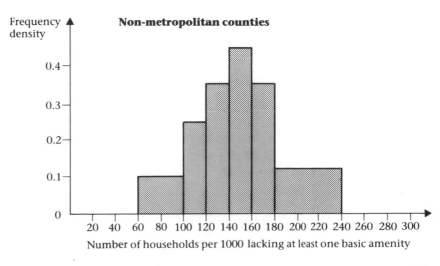

Number of households per 1000 lacking at least one basic amenity

119

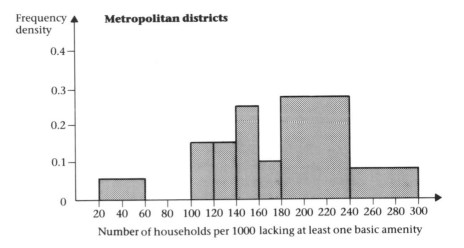

Frequency density — **Metropolitan districts**

Number of households per 1000 lacking at least one basic amenity

It is clear from the histogram that there is a much higher proportion of substandard housing in the metropolitan districts than in the non-metropolitan counties.

3.5 Averages and spread

> Confirm that, for this set of values, $\bar{x} = 4$ and the total of the square distances from the mean is 48.

$(1 + 2 + 2 + 3 + 5 + 6 + 9) \div 7 = 4$
$(1 - 4)^2 + (2 - 4)^2 + (2 - 4)^2 + (3 - 4)^2 + (5 - 4)^2 + (6 - 4)^2 + (9 - 4)^2 = 48$

> Find the mean and variance of the scores for each gymnast.

	First gymnast	Second gymnast
Mean	9.75	9.3
Variance	0.0025	0.17

The way these statistics are calculated is shown below for the first gymnast.

$$\text{mean, } \bar{x} = \frac{9.7 + 9.8 + 9.7 + 9.8 + 9.8 + 9.7}{6}$$

$$\text{variance} = \frac{(9.7 - 9.75)^2 + (9.8 - 9.75)^2 + (9.7 - 9.75)^2 + (9.8 - 9.75)^2 + (9.8 - 9.75)^2 + (9.7 - 9.75)^2}{6}$$

EXERCISE 2

1 (a) Mean = 54.2, standard deviation = 0.473 (both results to 3 s.f.)

   (b) New mean = 54.2 ÷ 1.10 = 49.3 (to 3 s.f).
       New standard deviation = 0.473 ÷ 1.10 = 0.430 (to 3 s.f.)

2 0.25 years.
   The standard deviation is unchanged.

3 Fahrenheit mean: $\frac{9}{5} \times 12 + 32 = 53.6\,°F$

   Fahrenheit standard deviation: $\frac{9}{5} \times 0.5 = 0.9\,°F$

3.7 Variance for frequency distributions

Calculate the mean and variance of this data set.

$$\bar{x} = \frac{14.3 \times 1 + 14.4 \times 3 + 14.5 \times 1}{5}$$

$$= 14.4$$

$$\text{Variance} = \frac{(14.3 - 14.4)^2 + 3(14.4 - 14.4)^2 + (14.5 - 14.4)^2}{5}$$

$$= 0.004$$

3.8 The mean and variance for grouped data

EXERCISE 3

1 (a) The mean is approximately 23.3 and the standard deviation is approximately 12.5.

   (b) The average length of rally has increased; coaching has been of some benefit!

2 (a) The total population is 53 511 000.

   (b) The population mean is approximately 41 years.

   (c) The population variance is approximately 580. Therefore, the standard deviation is approximately 24 years.

3 (a) The upper boundary must be taken somewhere! There are so few people aged over 100 that this seems a reasonable upper value.

(b) The mean is 38.1 years, standard deviation 22.9 years.

(c) The total population (50 063 000 in 1986) is expected to increase by about $3\frac{1}{2}$ million and the average age is expected to rise from 38 years to 41 years. There is little change in the spread of the ages.

4 (a) There is no obvious upper bound, such as that for age in question 3. You might, for example, consider it unlikely that a mortgage of more than £100 000 is taken.

Results will vary according to the size chosen for the first and last intervals. One possible grouping is given below.

Amount	Mid-value	First-time buyers	Other buyers
£ 5000–£9999	£7500	6	6
£10000–£13999	£12000	11	7
£14000–£17999	£16000	15	10
£18000–£21999	£20000	15	12
£22000–£24999	£23500	10	8
£25000–£29999	£27500	15	16
£30000–£99999	£65000	28	42

(b) Using the statistics mode on a calculator, the following results are obtained.

First-time buyers

The mean is approximately £31 845, which can be rounded to £32 000. The standard deviation is approximately £21 334, which you can round to £21 000.

The size chosen for the last interval makes the large standard deviation inevitable.

Other buyers

The mean is approximately £38 485, which you can round to £38 000. The standard deviation is approximately £22 925, which you can round to £23 000.

(c) Other buyers appear to obtain mortgages which are, on average, approximately £6000 higher than those of first-time buyers.

Former house owners are taking out higher mortgages, probably moving to more expensive houses. They are also taking out a greater range of mortgages, whereas first-time buyers are perhaps constrained to a narrower price bracket.

4 Probability models 1

4.2 Order from chaos

> Explain why the sum of the probabilities must equal 1.

The probability distribution is a listing of all of the events that can possibly happen, together with their probabilities. It is **certain** that one of the events **must** happen so that P(A) + P(B) + ... etc., must equal 1.

EXERCISE 1

1

s	1	2	3	4	5	6
P(s)	$\frac{1}{6}$	$\frac{1}{6}$	$\frac{1}{6}$	$\frac{1}{6}$	$\frac{1}{6}$	$\frac{1}{6}$

2

x	0	1	2	3	4 or over
P(x)	0.14	0.20	0.51	0.10	0.05

3

s	0	1
P(s)	$\frac{1}{2}$	$\frac{1}{2}$

4

y	1	2	3	4	5	6	7	8	9	10
P(y)	$\frac{1}{13}$	$\frac{1}{13}$	$\frac{1}{13}$	$\frac{1}{13}$	$\frac{1}{13}$	$\frac{1}{13}$	$\frac{1}{13}$	$\frac{1}{13}$	$\frac{1}{13}$	$\frac{4}{13}$

5

t	0–1	1–2	2–3	3 or over
P(t)	0.155	0.282	0.323	0.241

4.4 The mean and variance of a random variable

EXERCISE 2

1

d	1	2	3	4	5	6
$P(d)$	$\frac{1}{6}$	$\frac{1}{6}$	$\frac{1}{6}$	$\frac{1}{6}$	$\frac{1}{6}$	$\frac{1}{6}$

$$\mu = 1 \times \tfrac{1}{6} + 2 \times \tfrac{1}{6} + \ldots + 5 \times \tfrac{1}{6} + 6 \times \tfrac{1}{6} = 3.5$$
$$\sigma^2 = (1^2 \times \tfrac{1}{6} + 2^2 \times \tfrac{1}{6} + \ldots + 6^2 \times \tfrac{1}{6}) - 3.5^2$$
$$= 2.917$$

2

x	10	20	50
$P(x)$	0.4	0.4	0.2

Mean $(\mu) = 22$ pence
Variance $(\sigma^2) = 216$

3 (a)

x	1	2	3
$P(x)$	$\frac{1}{3}$	$\frac{1}{3}$	$\frac{1}{3}$

$\mu = 2$
$\sigma^2 = \frac{2}{3}$

(b)

x	0	1	2
$P(x)$	0.2	0.2	0.6

$\mu = 1.4$
$\sigma^2 = 0.64$

(c)

x	0	2	3	4
$P(x)$	$\frac{1}{3}$	$\frac{1}{6}$	$\frac{1}{3}$	$\frac{1}{6}$

$\mu = 2$
$\sigma^2 = 2\frac{1}{3}$

4

Score x	1	2	3	4	5	6	7	8	9	10
$P(x)$	$\frac{4}{52}$	$\frac{4}{52}$	$\frac{4}{52}$	$\frac{4}{52}$	$\frac{4}{52}$	$\frac{4}{52}$	$\frac{4}{52}$	$\frac{4}{52}$	$\frac{4}{52}$	$\frac{16}{52}$

Mean = 6.538,   variance = 9.94

5 The random variable is the journey time in minutes. The letter T would be an appropriate choice to denote this random variable.

t	15	20	45
$P(t)$	0.2	0.4	0.4

Mean journey time, $\mu = 29$ minutes

6 (a)

w	0	50	100	500	1000	5000
P(w)	0.9	8.355×10^{-5}	5.59×10^{-6}	1.30×10^{-6}	0.43×10^{-6}	1.35×10^{-8}

w	10000	25000	50000	100000	250000
P(w)	2.69×10^{-9}	2.16×10^{-9}	2.16×10^{-9}	2.16×10^{-9}	5.39×10^{-10}

(b) Mean (μ) = £0.0064

(c) The expected winnings per bond is £0.0064 × 12 or approximately 7.7p. A fixed interest account paying 10% would pay 10p over the year.

7 (a) Let X = expected gain

X	0	10	50
P(X)	0.5	0.25	0.25

$\mu = 0 \times 0.5 + 10 \times 0.25 + 50 \times 0.25 = 15\text{p}$

(b) The centre of the coin must land inside the square shown. As the target square is a quarter of the area of the square in total, the probability of this happening is 0.25. This reduces the probability of winning 10p or 50p by a quarter, so the expected gain is reduced to 3.75p.

5 Probability models 2

5.2 Adding probabilities

> Use the addition law to justify this last statement.

The events are 'late' or 'not late' – the bus cannot be both. Since one or the other event must happen,

$1 = $ P (late *or* not late)
   $= $ P (late) + P (not late) $-$ P (not late *and* late)
   $= $ P (late) + P (not late)

EXERCISE 1

1 (a) P(double six) = P(six) × P(six)

$$= \tfrac{1}{6} \times \tfrac{1}{6} = \tfrac{1}{36}$$

(b) P(at least one six) = $1 - $ P(no sixes)

$$= 1 - (\tfrac{5}{6})(\tfrac{5}{6}) = \tfrac{11}{36}$$

(c) P(one six) = P(six and no six) + P(no six and six)

$$= \tfrac{1}{6} \times \tfrac{5}{6} + \tfrac{5}{6} \times \tfrac{1}{6} = \tfrac{5}{18}$$

2 (a) P(red ace) = P(red) × P(ace)

$$= \tfrac{1}{2} \times \tfrac{4}{52} = \tfrac{1}{26}$$

(b) P(6 or 7) = P(6) + P(7)

$$= \tfrac{4}{52} + \tfrac{4}{52} = \tfrac{2}{13}$$

(c) P(ace or Queen) = P(ace) + P(Queen)

$$= \tfrac{1}{13} + \tfrac{1}{13} = \tfrac{2}{13}$$

3 (a) P(heart or six) = P(heart) + P(six) $-$ P(heart and six)

$$= \tfrac{13}{52} + \tfrac{4}{52} - \tfrac{1}{52} = \tfrac{4}{13}$$

(b) P(heart or spade) = P(heart) + P(spade)

$$= \tfrac{1}{4} + \tfrac{1}{4} = \tfrac{1}{2}$$

4 P(head) = $\tfrac{1}{2}$,   P(Jack) $= \tfrac{4}{52} = \tfrac{1}{13}$

(a) P(head or Jack) = $\tfrac{1}{2} + \tfrac{1}{13} - \tfrac{1}{2} \times \tfrac{1}{13}$
$$= \tfrac{7}{13}$$

(b) P(head and Jack) $= \tfrac{1}{2} \times \tfrac{1}{13} = \tfrac{1}{26}$

5.3   Tree diagrams

> Why can you multiply the probabilities in this case?

Because the events are independent – you want one event **and** the other, so you multiply.

> Why can you add these probabilities?

The events are mutually exclusive and cannot occur together. You want any one of them and so you add probabilities.

E X E R C I S E   2

1   P(no faults) = $0.8 \times 0.7 \times 0.9 = 0.504$

P(4 faults)   = 0.398

P(8 faults)   = $0.8 \times 0.3 \times 0.1 + 0.2 \times 0.7 \times 0.1 + 0.2 \times 0.3 \times 0.9$
                = 0.092

P(12 faults) = $0.2 \times 0.3 \times 0.1 = 0.006$

f	0	4	8	12
P($F = f$)	0.504	0.398	0.092	0.006

2

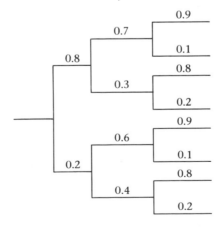

(a) P(no faults) = $0.8 \times 0.7 \times 0.9$
                    = 0.504

(b) P(4 faults)   = $0.8 \times 0.7 \times 0.1 + 0.8 \times 0.3 \times 0.8 + 0.2 \times 0.6 \times 0.9$
                    = 0.356

3 (a) (i) $\left(\dfrac{1}{4}\right)^3 = \dfrac{1}{64}$

(ii) Events HHH or DDD or SSS or CCC: P(same suit) $= 4 \times \left(\dfrac{1}{4}\right)^3 = \dfrac{1}{16}$

(b) (i) P(HHH) $= \dfrac{13}{52} \times \dfrac{12}{51} \times \dfrac{11}{50} = 0.0129$ (to 3 s.f.)

(ii) P(same suit) $= 4 \times 0.0129 = 0.0518$ (to 3 s.f.)

4

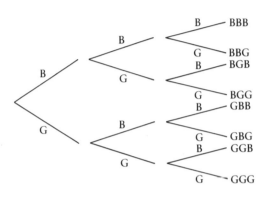

(a) Events BBG or BGB or GBB

P(one girl) $= \dfrac{3}{8}$

(b) P(at least one girl) $= 1 - $ P(no girls)

$$= 1 - \dfrac{1}{8} = \dfrac{7}{8}$$

(c) $1 - $ P(all boys or all girls) $= 1 - \left(\dfrac{1}{8} + \dfrac{1}{8}\right) = \dfrac{3}{4}$

5.4 The binostat

E X E R C I S E   3

1 (a) $\begin{pmatrix} 7 \\ 4 \end{pmatrix} = 35$ (b) 35   (c) 15   (d) 10

(e) 2   (f) 35   (g) 5   (h) 1

2 (a) Exactly 3 heads can be obtained in 35 ways.

(b) Exactly 4 tails can be obtained in 35 ways.

If exactly 3 heads are obtained in 7 throws then exactly 4 tails must also occur. This tells you that $\binom{7}{3}$ and $\binom{7}{4}$ must be equal.

3   There are $\binom{8}{6}$ ways of cutting 6 red cards out of 8 cuts.

Each way has probability $\left(\dfrac{1}{2}\right)^6 \times \left(\dfrac{1}{2}\right)^2$ so the probability of cutting a red card 6 times out of 8 is

$$\binom{8}{6} \times \left(\frac{1}{2}\right)^6 \times \left(\frac{1}{2}\right)^2 = 28 \times \frac{1}{256} = 0.109 \quad \text{(to 3 s.f.)}$$

4   The probability of the family containing 4 girls is

$$\left(\frac{1}{2}\right)^4 = \frac{1}{16}$$

There are $\binom{4}{3}$ ways of having 3 girls in a family of 4, so the probability of the family containing precisely 3 girls is

$$4 \times \frac{1}{16} = \frac{1}{4}$$

The probability of the family containing 3 or more girls is therefore

$$\frac{1}{16} + \frac{1}{4} = \frac{5}{16}$$

5   (a) The probability all 5 neutrons are absorbed is

$$\left(\frac{1}{2}\right)^5 = \frac{1}{32}$$

(b) The probability 3 neutrons are absorbed is

$$\binom{5}{3} \times \left(\frac{1}{2}\right)^5 = \frac{5}{16}$$

6   The probability that 5 draw red and 5 draw white is

$$\binom{10}{5} \times \left(\frac{1}{2}\right)^{10} = 252 \times \frac{1}{1024}$$

$$= 0.246 \text{ (to 3 s.f.)}$$

5.5   Unequal probabilities

E X E R C I S E   4

1 S = the number of sixes when 4 dice are thrown

The probability of no sixes $= \dfrac{5}{6} \times \dfrac{5}{6} \times \dfrac{5}{6} \times \dfrac{5}{6}$

The probability of 1 six $= \dbinom{4}{1} \times \dfrac{1}{6} \times \dfrac{5}{6} \times \dfrac{5}{6} \times \dfrac{5}{6}$

The probability of 2 sixes $= \dbinom{4}{2} \times \dfrac{1}{6} \times \dfrac{1}{6} \times \dfrac{5}{6} \times \dfrac{5}{6}$

The probability of 3 sixes $= \dbinom{4}{3} \times \dfrac{1}{6} \times \dfrac{1}{6} \times \dfrac{1}{6} \times \dfrac{5}{6}$

The probability of 4 sixes $= \dbinom{4}{4} \times \dfrac{1}{6} \times \dfrac{1}{6} \times \dfrac{1}{6} \times \dfrac{1}{6}$

S	0	1	2	3	4
P(S)	0.482	0.386	0.116	0.015	0.001

2   The probability that Bob misses the board is $\frac{1}{3}$. The probability that he hits the board is therefore $\frac{2}{3}$.

The probability that none land on the board is

$$\dfrac{1}{3} \times \dfrac{1}{3} \times \dfrac{1}{3}$$

The probability that 1 lands on the board is

$$\dbinom{3}{1} \times \dfrac{2}{3} \times \dfrac{1}{3} \times \dfrac{1}{3} \text{ and so on.}$$

D	0	1	2	3
P(D)	0.037	0.222	0.444	0.296

3   (a)   If Wizzo is no better or worse than Wow then the probability that 1 person prefers Wizzo is $\frac{1}{2}$.

The probability that exactly 8 prefer Wizzo $= \dbinom{10}{8} \times \left(\dfrac{1}{2}\right)^{10} = 0.044$

The probability that 9 prefer Wizzo $= \binom{10}{9} \times \left(\frac{1}{2}\right)^{10} = 0.010$

The probability that all 10 prefer Wizzo $= 1 \times \left(\frac{1}{2}\right)^{10} = 0.001$

So the probability of 8 or more is $0.044 + 0.010 + 0.001 = 0.055$.

(b) The probability that exactly 8 prefer Wizzo $= \binom{10}{8} \times (0.8)^8 \times (0.2)^2$

$$= 0.302$$

The probability that 9 prefer Wizzo $= \binom{10}{9} \times (0.8)^9 \times (0.2) = 0.268$

The probability that all 10 prefer Wizzo $= 1 \times (0.8)^{10} = 0.107$

The total probability of 8 or more is $0.302 + 0.268 + 0.107 = 0.677$.

4 The probability of 3 girls $= \binom{4}{3} \times (0.48)^3 \times (0.52) = 0.230$

The probability of 4 girls $= 1 \times (0.48)^4 = 0.053$

Thus the probability that a family of 4 contains 3 or more girls is

$0.230 + 0.053 = 0.283$

5 The probability that Cambridge win 3 out of 5

$= \binom{5}{3} \times (0.46)^3 \times (0.54)^2$

$= 0.284$ (to 3 s.f.)

Since what happens in one year could influence the next (there may be the same teams for example) the assumption of independence is very weak. It is likely that the probability of Cambridge's success is **not** the same each year.

5.6   Making inferences

EXERCISE 5

1 (a) Probability of throwing 3 aces $= \binom{5}{3} \times \left(\frac{1}{6}\right)^3 \times \left(\frac{5}{6}\right)^2 = 0.0322$

Probability of throwing 4 aces $= \binom{5}{4} \times \left(\frac{1}{6}\right)^4 \times \left(\frac{5}{6}\right) = 0.0032$

Probability of throwing 5 aces $= 1 \times \left(\frac{1}{6}\right)^5 = 0.0001$

The total probability of 3 or more aces

$= 0.0322 + 0.0032 + 0.0001 = 0.0355$

(b) Probability of the result above 3 or more times out of 4 is

$$\binom{4}{3} \times (0.0355)^3 \times (0.9645) + (0.0355)^4 = 0.00017 \text{ (to 2 s.f.)}$$

This is an extremely unlikely event, so you should doubt the player's honesty.

2   Probability of winning 9 or more times out of $10 = 10 \times \left(\frac{1}{2}\right)^{10} + \left(\frac{1}{2}\right)^{10}$

$$= 0.0107 \text{ (to 3 s.f.)}$$

The captain is therefore extremely lucky.

3   Probability of rain on 6 or more days out of 7 is

$$\binom{7}{6} \times \left(\frac{1}{3}\right)^6 \times \left(\frac{2}{3}\right) + \left(\frac{1}{3}\right)^7 = 0.0069 \text{ (to 2 s.f.)}$$

The Wilsons were very unlucky with the weather. The model is almost certainly not appropriate – the assumption of independence is weak.

4   If both drinks were the same you would expect the probability that 7 or more out of 8 would prefer the new flavour to be

$$\binom{8}{7} \times \left(\frac{1}{2}\right)^8 + \left(\frac{1}{2}\right)^8 = 0.0352 \text{ (to 3 s.f.)}$$

This result is clearly unlikely and suggests that the new flavour is preferred.

5   (a) The probability that at least one seed will germinate out of the five planted is the same as

1 – probability that **none** of the seeds germinate $= 1 - (0.8)^5$
$$= 0.67232$$

(b) $1 - (0.8)^n = 0.9$
$$0.1 = (0.8)^n$$

This can be solved by 'trial and improving' on a calculator, or you can take natural logarithms of both sides,

$$\ln(0.1) = n \ln(0.8)$$

$$n = \frac{\ln(0.1)}{\ln(0.8)}$$

$$n = 10.3$$

Thus 11 or more seeds must be planted to ensure a 90% chance of at least one germination.

6 Sampling.

6.2 Bias in sampling

> Can you explain this curious result?

As the same number of trains run east as west the answer must have something to do with the time the trains arrive at the station.

Suppose the westbound trains arrives 10 minutes after the eastbound train. The following diagram should help to explain the paradox in the case when eastbound trains arrive on the hour, every hour.

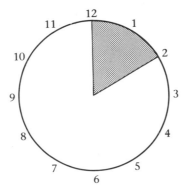

There are ten minutes when the next train will be westbound (shaded) and fifty minutes when the next train will be eastbound (unshaded).

> How could the princess legitimately improve her favourite's chances and what precisely would his chances then be?

The princess ensures that her favourite suitor's coin is in one of the urns on its own. All the other suitors' coins are in the second urn. The king has a 50:50 chance of choosing the urn with the princess' favourite suitor's coin.

EXERCISE 1

1 The sample is biased.

If you assume that each floor is equally populated, then the lift is more likely to be above floor 3 than below floor 3. Similarly, the lift is more likely to be below the 10th floor than above it.

2 The sample is biased.

Possible reasons are:

(a) One elderly person with a contagious disease is more likely to pass it on to another elderly person in the residential home than if he or she were living alone.

133

(b) People in a residential home are more likely to be in need of medical attention.

(c) Elderly people living in a residential home are likely to have better living conditions (food, heating etc.) than those not living in a residential home.

(d) If the home is fee-paying then residents are unlikely to be representative of the general population.

3   The sample was biased.

Truman in fact won the 1948 US Presidential Election. The incorrect forecast of the opinion poll was attributed to the fact that the majority of telephone owners in the US in 1948 were Republican voters. Those who owned telephones did not form a representative sample of the voting population.

4   The sample is biased.

In November the main reason for absences is likely to be illness. Truancy and interviews are more likely to be reasons in the spring and summer terms.

6.3   Sample size

> What useful information can be obtained from a sample of one?

Not a great deal – clearly the more information you obtain, the better able you are to make inferences about the population.

> Why would you expect a sample of 20 to be better still?

The means of samples of size 20 are more clustered around the population mean than the means of smaller samples. Consequently, the mean of a sample of 20 is more likely to be close to the actual population mean than the mean of a smaller sample.

6.4   Testing claims by simulation

> (a) Which people would you expect to be in favour of a monorail in the centre of a city?
>
> (b) How many replied and of those who replied, how many wanted
>
>   (i) the monorail   (ii) the trams   (iii) neither?

(a) You would expect those who regularly commute to the centre to be in favour – also perhaps shop owners.

(b) A total of 48 replied.   (i) 5   (ii) 23   (iii) 20

(a) What do you understand the word 'bias' to mean?

(b) How do you think the monorail 'poll' was carried out? Would this method introduce bias in the sample? Suggest a better method.

(a) A dictionary might define a bias as a predisposition or prejudice. Thus a die is biased if it is predisposed to show a particular face more than any other. A telephone poll is predisposed to selecting relatively prosperous members of society.

(b) A sampling procedure ideally should be just as likely to choose one particular member of the population as it is any other but often this is impracticable.

The sample of 48 were, in fact, the people who filled in a coupon accompanying a previous article on the monorail proposal. Such a sampling procedure is almost bound to introduce bias. In this case, it could be argued that people opposed to new proposals are much more likely to take the trouble to write in than people who feel favourably about them. A better method would be to conduct a random sample of the population of the city and its surrounding districts.

6.5   Further testing

Why is a binomial model suitable for this situation?

You should assume

(a) that the dogs do not influence each other and make their choice of food **independently** of the other dogs;

(b) the dogs either choose the food or they do not (i.e. there are only two possible outcomes of a dog choosing). These assumptions are necessary for a binomial model.

What is the probability that 8 or more dogs in a sample of 10 will choose Wolfit?

$$\frac{45}{1024} + \frac{10}{1024} + \frac{1}{1024} = \frac{56}{1024} = 0.055 \text{ (to 2 s.f.)}$$

EXERCISE 2

1

(a) P(6 correct) $= \binom{8}{6}\left(\frac{1}{2}\right)^6\left(\frac{1}{2}\right)^2$

$= 28 \left(\frac{1}{2}\right)^8$

$= \frac{28}{256}(\approx 11\%)$

(b) P(6 or more) $= \binom{8}{6}\left(\frac{1}{2}\right)^8 + \binom{8}{7}\left(\frac{1}{2}\right)^8 + \binom{8}{8}\left(\frac{1}{2}\right)^8$

$= \frac{28}{256} + \frac{8}{256} + \frac{1}{256}$

$= \frac{37}{256}\left(\approx 14\%\right)$

Random guessing would produce a result of 6 or more correct 'predictions' in about 14% of cases. 7 or 8 correct results would have been more convincing.

2 From the table in the test:

P(7 or more correct) $= \frac{120 + 45 + 10 + 1}{1024} = \frac{176}{1024}$ $(\approx 17\%)$

P(8 or more correct) $= \frac{45 + 10 + 1}{1024} = \frac{56}{1024}$ $(\approx 5\%)$

P(9 or more correct) $= \frac{10 + 1}{1024} = \frac{11}{1024}$ $(\approx 1\%)$

8 or more correct is quite convincing. 9 or 10 correct would make you more certain that they are not guessing.